Flavors of Italy

Flavors of Italy

MARIAPAOLA DETTORE

SICILY

TIME
LIFE
BOOKS

TIME-LIFE BOOKS IS A DIVISION OF TIME LIFE INC.

TIME-LIFE BOOKS
President and CEO   George Artandi

TIME-LIFE CUSTOM PUBLISHING
Vice President and Publisher   Terry Newell
Vice President of Sales and Marketing   Neil Levin
Editor for Special Markets   Anna Burgard
Director of Special Sales   Liz Ziehl

TIME-LIFE is a trademark of Time Warner Inc. U.S.A.
Library of Congress Cataloging-in Publication Data
Dettore, Mariapaola.
    Sicily: culinary traditions from the Sicilian provinces / by Mariapaola
Dettore; with photography by Marco Lanza.
    p. cm. -- (Flavors of Italy)
    Includes index.
    ISBN 0-7370-0012-0
    1. Cookery, Italian--Sicilian style. 2. Cookery--Italy--Sicily.
I. Title. II. Series.
TX723.2.S55D48 1999   98-52936
641.59458--DC21   CIP
                         r98

Copyright © McRae Books Srl 1999

This book was conceived, edited and designed by McRae Books Srl, Florence Italy.
Text: Mariapaola Dettore   Photography: Marco Lanza
Set Design: Rosalba Gioffré   Design: Marco Nardi
Translation from the Italian: Sara Harris   Editing: Anne McRae,
(in association with First Edition)   Mollie Thomson, Alison Leach

Color separations: Fotolito Toscana, Florence, Italy
Printed and bound in Italy by Grafiche Editoriali Padane

Cover photographs: Front cover, Index Stock Photography, Inc.
Back cover, counterclockwise from top left: Milo Minnella, Marco Lanza, Adriano Nardi, Marco Lanza,
Giuliano Cappelli, Marco Lanza

Cover design: WorkHorse Creative

Contents

Introduction

Sicily lies at the very heart of the Mediterranean, its shores washed by three seas: the Ionian, the Tyrrhenian, and the Mediterranean. Because of its central location, the island has been a melting pot of peoples and civilizations since the earliest times. This, combined with the mild climate, the fertility of the land, and the abundant stocks of fish in the surrounding waters, have all contributed to the extremely varied and unique flavor of Sicilian cuisine.

The Doric temple at Segesta (built 5th century BC) still stands as a reminder of the Greek presence in Sicily. The Greeks strongly influenced the island's gastronomic history, by introducing several types of bread; various ways of processing olives to be eaten with the bread; the salting of ricotta cheese (so that it kept for longer and had a variety of flavors and uses); and honey (and, in consequence, bee-keeping). The Greeks probably also introduced wine, although what was produced was of inferior quality for many centuries. As with other wine-producing countries, viticulture in Sicily had a checkered history until the science of wine-making was more fully understood.

Sicilian cooking closely reflects the island's history. Its gastronomic tradition was built up gradually in a series of layers, as wave upon wave of conquerors and immigrants were assimilated into the life of the island. Around 700 BC Sicily was colonized by the Phoenicians in the west of the island and by the Greeks in the east. During this early period some very talented local cooks recorded their recipes in cook books; sadly, only fragments of these have survived.

In 241 BC Sicily became the first Roman province and was known throughout the classical world as Rome's granary. The Romans built theaters in Syracuse and Taormina on the sites where Greek theaters had stood, and villas: the Roman villa of Casale, near Piazza Armerina is famous for its superb mosaics. Sicily's economy did not benefit greatly from the Roman occupation, although there was an increase in fishing and sheep-rearing. The area around Taormina also became famous for the quality of its wine and the port of Palermo (the chief port for grain shipments to Rome) grew very important.

With the fall of the Roman Empire in the 5th century, the island fell prey to the Franks and Goths and to a real decline in economic fortunes.

Mosaic with fishermen from the Roman hunting lodge near Piazza Armerina in Sicily. Roman influence in culinary matters survives in such dishes as Maccu di Fave *(see recipe, page 31), in the practice of stuffing fish and vegetables, in the art of sausage-making and, almost certainly, in the technique of storing snow from Mount Etna (which persisted until refrigerators were introduced). The Romans of mainland Italy are known to have stored snow in underground pits so that they could enjoy refreshingly cold, fruit-based concoctions during the hot summer months.*

The Byzantines were next in this inexorable succession of occupying powers and it was some three hundred years before they in turn were driven out, leaving behind them a considerable artistic legacy. Their contribution to Sicilian cooking was confined to the introduction of some new spices, the practice of spit-roasting large cuts of meat, and more sophisticated techniques for maturing cheeses to increase their strength, flavor, and keeping qualities.

The Arabs or Saracens were the next rulers of Sicily and their influence on its culinary history was profound (see pages 82–83).

In the mid-11th century, the Normans took possession of the island and established the Kingdom of Sicily, which included a large part of southern Italy. During the reign of Frederick II, who was an enlightened ruler and a great patron of the arts and sciences, cultural life experienced a golden age, centered on his court in Palermo. At this time, Sicilian cooking was still predominantly Siculo-Arab in character, but other, new foodstuffs were being imported for the first time as international commerce expanded.

Sicilian products were bartered with merchants from northern Europe in exchange for preserved fish: smoked or salted herrings, salt cod, and stockfish. These were landed at the port of Messina, where *Stockfish Messina-Style* is still a typical local dish (see recipe, page 88).

As the 14th century progressed, Sicilian cooking became richer and more elaborate, influenced by its Spanish rulers from the House of Aragon. All sorts of fried foods became popular, while the nuns in various convents created new cakes and sweetmeats, probably to satisfy a demand from the ruling aristocratic families. Some of these recipes, such as the extraordinary *Cassata di Erice* and *Frutta di Martorana* (see page 21) are still very popular. *Farsumaru* (see recipe, page 62) also dates from this era. It is often known as *rollò*, a corruption of the French word *rouleau*, a legacy from the time when Sicily looked to France for culinary leadership. Other words confirm this tendency; for example, *gattò* (from *gateau*) and *ragù* (from *ragout*). The Sicilian version of *ragù* (meat sauce) is, in fact, much closer to the original French recipe than the one served in mainland Italy.

During this period trade with the Middle East and the arrival of Jewish immigrants brought the eggplant (aubergine) to Sicily. Long an ingredient of Arab and Jewish cooking, eggplants originated in China and India. Although it was many years before they were appreciated in other European countries, the Sicilians immediately adopted them and incorporated them into their culinary repertoire. Fried, stuffed, broiled (grilled), preserved in oil, served with rice and pasta dishes, or in the famous *Capunata* (see recipe, page 24), they still play an important part in countless dishes.

Under the rule of the Sicilian branch of the House of Aragon (1412–1713), new foodstuffs arrived in Europe from America: tomatoes, bell peppers (capsicums), maize, potatoes, beans (although one variety, native to Africa and Asia, the black-eyed bean, had been known since Greek and Roman times), cocoa, vanilla, and many others. Many were met with understandable suspicion and error: in one instance, people thought that potato leaves were edible, only to discover that the solanine they contained was poisonous!

Sponge cake, the fatless version used in *Cassata* (see recipe, page 108), and other delicacies, is said to have been invented by an unknown Sicilian pastrycook experimenting with a mixture of eggs, sugar, and flour.

Sicily continued to be governed by a succession of foreign powers: it was handed over to the House of Savoy, then ruled by the Bourbon Kings of Naples, and finally subsumed into the Kingdom of Italy, thereafter following the fortunes of the mainland. None of these changes was of any great benefit to the Sicilian economy, nor did they have much influence on the island's cuisine, which was by then well established with its own, very distinctive and ineradicable character.

The Spanish presence enriched Sicilian life with a certain magnificence, an extravagantly baroque, lavish quality. In culinary terms, however, the island underwent little change under Aragonese rule, although different, more playful, and sometimes grandiose names were given to existing dishes, replacing their less pretentious ones in the local dialect. Sicilian cooks exploited the rich and well-established repertoire of local specialties to satisfy the demands of their aristocratic employers, while also taking every opportunity to be creative by experimenting and trying out new ideas.

With the exception of certain local specialties, modern Sicilian cooking does not vary tremendously from one part of the island to another. It relies heavily on five basic elements: pasta, fish, cheese, vegetables, and patisserie.

Pasta is ubiquitous, with an inexhaustible variety of sauces. Fresh pasta used to be made at home, with hard (durum) wheat flour, water, salt, and plenty of painstaking and energetic preparation. The resulting dough was shaped in a variety of ways, the most famous being *macaroni*. A thin metal skewer, reed, or length of cane, was pushed through small pieces of dough and these were then skillfully pressed out along the skewer to about a hand's span in length; the skewer was then extracted, producing a fairly thick spaghetti with a hole in the middle. There are a wide variety of fresh and dried ribbon noodles, usually made from egg pasta sheets, ranging from the slender *tagliolini* to *lasagne* and *cannelloni*. Nowadays most cooks use industrially produced pasta but, on special occasions, certain types of pasta are still freshly made by hand.

Today Sicily produces some good quality beef and over the last 10–20 years butter has, for the first time in history, found its way into Sicilian cooking, although olive oil is still far more widely used.

Pork has always played a more important role than beef and there is a splendid variety of fresh sausages, and a more restricted but interesting range of cured, sliceable sausages, especially in eastern Sicily.

Sheep and goats have always been reared in most parts of Sicily and dishes with lamb and kid (see recipes, pages 68, 69, 72) are traditional and typical of the local cooking. Goat's milk and ewe's milk are used to make cheeses, from the deliciously mild, almost sweet, ricotta so widely used by pastrycooks, and the bland, white tuma, to *canestrati* cheeses which bear the imprint of the wicker molds in which they are drained and shaped. These are described at greater length in the section on cheeses (see pages 40–41).

The regions of Sicily are shown on this loaf of bread baked for the Festa del Pane *(Bread Festival) held on St. Joseph's Day, at Salemi, in the province of Trapani.*

An old windmill at a flour factory is being restored in the province of Trapani.

Surrounded by three seas, it is not surprising that Sicily boasts a wealth of fish dishes.

For the visitor to the picturesque Vuccirìa market in the heart of old Palermo, set in a maze of alleyways dating from the time of Spanish rule, there awaits a dazzling array of fruits, vegetables, and fish of every conceivable type. The mouthwatering aroma of crisply fried foods such as Panelle di Ciciri *(see recipe, page 22),* Arancini *(see recipe, page 18), potato croquettes, known as* Cazzilli, *fritters of baby globe artichokes, cardoons, cauliflower, and eggplants. Not to mention the special* Pagnottelle, *freshly baked rolls with all sorts of fillings, served piping hot.*

Trapani, a port on the west coast of Sicily, is renowned for its tuna fishing. One of the products of this industry is *bottarga*, the pressed, salted, and dried roe of tuna fish, which is served in thin slices dressed with olive oil, lemon juice, freshly gound pepper, and, sometimes, finely chopped parsley. Wafer-thin slices of filleted tuna and dolphin are processed and served in the same way. Another specialty of Trapani is *cucusu* or couscous (served with fish) of Arabic origin which came from North Africa long ago.

Messina, on the north-eastern tip of Sicily, is synonymous with swordfish, large numbers of which are caught in the Straits of Messina during the spring and early summer. It is prepared in all sorts of ways: as broiled (grilled) swordfish steaks with lemon sauce (see recipe, page 85), coated in egg and breadcrumbs and fried, and made into a soup called *ghiotta*. This busy port is also renowned for *Piscistuocco a Ghiotta* (see recipe, page 88).

Sardines are plentiful in all Sicilian coastal waters and, as with tuna, there is a flourishing canning industry. Freshly landed sardines are stuffed and rolled (see recipe, page 76). But the most famous Sicilian sardine dish is pasta with sardines (see recipe, page 38) which comes from **Palermo** but is served in many parts of the island. Palermo's cuisine offers tremendous variety, particularly in the preparation of vegetables. There is a wide choice of first courses (*Risu a Palermitana*, see recipe, page 32), main courses such as the classic *Farsumaru* (see recipe, page 62), and interesting fish dishes, including *Murruzzi a Palermitana* (see recipe, page 78).

Continuing this gastronomic tour through Sicily and crossing to the east of the island, **Catania**'s specialties include the deservedly famous *Pasta al a Norma* (see recipe, page 29), and the superb anchovies which are landed nearby and prepared in all sorts of ways. In one dish (see recipe, page 74), they are baked in the oven with olives and pine nuts.

Syracuse and **Ragusa**, in the south-east, are known for their fresh, well-prepared fish dishes. Ragusa is noted for the quality of its pecorino and ricotta cheeses, while the fertile land around Syracuse produces excellent citrus fruit and some of the island's finest vegetables.

In **Agrigento**, vegetables are also outstanding for their freshness and flavor. Fresh, locally made spicy sausages are of note; there are several recipes for casseroles of kid, and some very good cheeses are produced. Cakes, desserts, and confectionery are particularly good in this region.

The olive groves around the inland city of **Caltanissetta** produce very high quality olive oil, and the area is noted for its cheeses. Game plays an important part in the local cuisine: hares, wild rabbits, partridges, and, during the migration season, duck. Almond trees produce plenty of nuts for a variety of sweetmeats: the delectable *torrone*, two basic types of which are made, one being nougat, the other nougatine, while the local specialty, called *Tocchetti*, is a sliced, multicolored version of *torrone*.

Enna, situated on the edge of a high plateau in the center of Sicily, surrounded by the Ebrodi and Madonie mountains, has retained the island's most ancient culinary traditions and its cooking makes copious use of spices and robust sweet-sour flavors. A local specialty is *Piacintinu*, a cheese made from ewe's milk mixed with whole black peppercorns and saffron which colors it sunshine yellow. In common with the rest of Sicily, the inhabitants of Enna are spoiled for choice when it comes to patisserie and confectionery.

The rocks of Scylla and Charybdis near Catania, where Homer's hero Odysseus braved the sea monsters during a storm and went on to land on the island of the Sun, Thrinakia (the ancient name for Sicily).

In the central province of Enna, there is an intriguing recipe for Sicilian-style cutlets *which are not cutlets at all but slices of lean meat, briefly marinated in vinegar, drained, and covered with a mixture of grated cheese, garlic, and parsley, then dipped in beaten egg, coated with breadcrumbs and fried in olive oil. The fort at Cerere, shown below, dates from medieval times.*

Antipasti

Eating habits have changed in Sicily, as they have all over Italy. The *antipasti*, or appetizers, prepared by Sicilians today used to be (and often still are) served on their own as snacks or as side dishes with the main course. Try serving a selection, or all, of the recipes in this chapter in small quantities (as cocktail party food, for example); they provide a mouthwatering foretaste of the distinctive aromas and nuance of flavors which are so typical of Sicilian cooking.

Caciu all'Argintera

Hot Cheese and Herb Appetizer

Serves 4
Preparation: 2 minutes
Cooking: 6–7 minutes
Recipe grading: easy

Pour the oil into a wide, nonstick skillet. Add the garlic and cook over a low heat until pale golden brown. ❧ Place the cheese slices in the skillet in a single layer, increase the heat and cook, turning several times with a spatula. ❧ Sprinkle the cheese with the vinegar, oregano, and pepper. Cover and cook for 2 minutes more. ❧ Serve very hot.

- 4 tablespoons extra-virgin olive oil
- 2–3 cloves garlic, slightly crushed
- 4 slices fresh caciocavallo or fresh pecorino cheese, at least $^1/_2$ in/1 cm thick
- 2 tablespoons Italian red wine vinegar
- 1 teaspoon oregano, chopped
- freshly ground black pepper

Suggested wine: a dry red (Sciacca)

Legend has it that a silversmith in Palermo who had more talent for cooking than for business invented this simple but deliciously tasty snack or starter.

Pomodori Gratinati

Stuffed Baked Tomatoes

Serves 4
Cooking: 35 minutes
Preparation: 10 minutes
Recipe grading: easy

- 8 medium-large ripe tomatoes
- salt to taste
- freshly ground black pepper
- 2 medium onions, finely chopped
- 2 cloves garlic, finely chopped
- 2 tablespoons extra-virgin olive oil
- 4 tablespoons breadcrumbs
- 8 black olives, pitted and chopped
- 1 tablespoon pine nuts
- 1 tablespoon raisins
- 1 tablespoon capers

Suggested wine: a dry white (Corvo)

Rinse the tomatoes under cold running water and pat dry with paper towels. ❧ Cut the tough pithy core from the top of each tomato. Use a teaspoon to scoop out the flesh and juice and place in a bowl. Sprinkle the whole tomatoes with salt and pepper. ❧ Sauté the onion and garlic in the oil until transparent, then add the tomato flesh and juice and cook for a few minutes until it reduces a little. ❧ Remove from the heat and stir in the breadcrumbs, olives, pine nuts, raisins, and capers. ❧ Spoon the mixture into the tomatoes and place in an oiled ovenproof dish. ❧ Bake in a preheated oven at 350°F/180°C/gas 4 for 30 minutes. ❧ Serve hot or cold.

'Nsalata di Portualla
Orange Salad

Serves 4
Cooking: none
Preparation: 15 minutes
Recipe grading: easy

Peel the oranges, removing all the white pith as well as the skin. ❧ Slice them thinly or cut into small pieces. Place in a salad bowl and add the olives, leeks or chives, parsley, oil, salt and pepper. ❧ Toss gently but thoroughly and leave to stand for 10 minutes, then stir again and serve.

- 4 ripe, juicy oranges
- 8–10 green or black olives, pitted and cut into quarters
- 1 medium leek, cleaned, trimmed and thinly sliced into rings, or 4 tablespoons finely chopped chives
- 1 tablespoon finely chopped parsley
- 4 tablespoons extra-virgin olive oil
- salt to taste
- freshly ground black or white pepper

Suggested wine: a dry sparkling white (Corvo)

A salad full of surprises. Oranges served with oil and pepper are excellent with roast meats, especially when these are slightly fatty. This sophisticated version makes a very original, refreshing appetizer.

Arancini

Stuffed Rice Ball Fritters

Serves 4

Preparation: 40 minutes

Cooking: 30 minutes

Recipe grading: fairly easy

- 1½ cups/10 oz/300 g Italian Arborio rice
- ¾ cup/3½ oz/100 g fresh or frozen peas
- 3 tablespoons extra-virgin olive oil
- 1 tablespoon water
- 1 tablespoon onion, finely chopped
- 5 oz/150 g ground lean veal
- salt to taste
- freshly ground black pepper
- ½ cup/4 oz/125 g canned tomatoes
- ¼ teaspoon saffron, dissolved in 1 tablespoon of warm water
- 2 large eggs
- ½ cup/2 oz/60 g freshly grated mature, hard pecorino cheese
- 4 oz/125 g unmatured (semi-hard, sliceable) pecorino cheese or mozzarella cheese, cut into cubes
- a little all-purpose/plain flour
- 1–2 eggs, beaten
- 1½ cups/3 oz/90 g fresh breadcrumbs
- extra-virgin (or ordinary, good quality) olive oil for frying

Suggested wine: a young, medium rosé (Etna rosato)

The popularity of these "little oranges" with their crisp exterior over moist rice and a delicious filling has spread far beyond Sicily where they are popular as fresh "fast food" and also as a first course.

Cook the rice in boiling salted water until *al dente*. Drain and cool. ❧ Boil the peas in salted water for 2 minutes. Drain and place in a small saucepan with 1 tablespoon of the oil and the water. Cover tightly and cook for 4–5 minutes. ❧ Sauté the onion in the remaining oil. Add the veal and cook for 2 minutes over a slightly higher heat, using a fork to break up any lumps. ❧ Season with salt and pepper. Add the tomatoes and cook for 20 minutes or until very thick, then add the peas. ❧ Stir the saffron liquid into the eggs. Mix well with the rice and grated cheese. ❧ Take a heaped tablespoonful of the rice mixture in your palm and make a hollow with your thumb large enough to hold 1 tablespoon of the meat filling and a cube of cheese. Cover with another tablespoon of rice and shape into a compact ball the size of a small orange. ❧ Roll the "oranges" in flour, coat with beaten egg and roll in breadcrumbs. ❧ Deep-fry in very hot oil until golden brown. ❧ Drain and serve hot or at room temperature.

Aulivi Cunsati
Piquant Marinated Olives

Serves 4

Preparation: 15 minutes + several
  hours' standing time

Cooking: none

Recipe grading: easy

Pit the olives and press them with the heel of your hand to crush slightly. ✑ Put them into a bowl and add all the remaining ingredients. ✑ Stir well, then leave to stand for several hours before serving to let the flavors penetrate. ✑ They will keep for up to a week if stored in a tightly closed container in the refrigerator. ✑ For a slightly different but equally delicious dish, prepare the olives Syracuse-style, by adding 1 tablespoon of capers, a handful of chopped mint leaves, and a finely chopped heart of crisp green celery.

- 2 cups, tightly packed/10 oz/300 g mild green olives, pickled in brine
- 1–2 cloves garlic, thinly sliced
- 1 small chili pepper, seeded and finely chopped
- 3½ tablespoons extra-virgin olive oil
- 1 tablespoon wine vinegar
- 2½ teaspoons chopped oregano

Suggested wine: a dry red
  (Cerasuolo)

Olives play a very important role in Sicilian cooking. They are served in many ways, either on their own as appetizers or to add flavor to a wide variety of dishes.

Almonds

The sight of almond trees in blossom, like fluffy white or pink-tinged clouds, in the Valley of the Temples near Agrigento, is an unforgettable one. Across this peaceful valley are scattered the remains (some still standing) of magnificent temples dedicated to the gods and goddesses of classical antiquity: Juno, Jove, Hercules, Castor and Pollux, and Vulcan. Echoes of a bygone world still linger in the fields and almond groves, particularly in the dappled light of early spring when the almond trees blossom (and when they are sometimes caught by a late, unexpected frost).

The ancient gods are long since forgotten, but the almonds are still very much in use. Many different varieties are grown, including sweet, bitter, hard-shelled, semi-hard shelled, and soft-shelled. They are widely used in Sicilian cooking, in dishes ranging from sauces to braised and casseroled meat, poultry, game, fish, and desserts. They are also used in drinks, such as almond milk, which is made with sweet almonds, orange flower water, and a tiny amount of specially treated bitter almonds.

Almonds are native to southwestern Asia from where they were introduced to Sicily. The almond tree is closely related to the peach and the two are quite similar in appearance.

Almonds reign supreme in patisserie and confectionery. They are the most important ingredients in an incredibly wide range of cookies, cakes, jams, candy, and nougat. When ground and mixed with sugar and orange flower water or vanilla they are transformed into the ever versatile marzipan, used raw for modeling or cooked and made into petits fours.

Uncooked marzipan, shaped into an enormous variety of tiny fruits, becomes a candy called Frutta di Martorana. *This candy became famous in the 14th century under the House of Aragon, when it was made by the sisters of a Benedictine order founded in Palermo by Heloise Martorana. Traditionally eaten in Palermo as a Sunday treat, it is now a favorite of pastrycooks all over the island.*

Marzipan is also shaped into little Easter treats – miniature lambs, pigs, donkeys, and horses – the animal varies from village to village. Another type of richly decorated candy, called the Easter Heart, is given to family and friends as a token of affection. A soft marzipan, called pasta reale *or "royal almond paste" is used in the very elaborate* Erice Cassata, *which also includes citron jelly as part of its filling.*

Panelle di Ciciri
Garbanzo Bean Fritters

Serves 4
Preparation: 3 minutes
Cooking: 40 minutes + cooling time
Recipe grading: easy

- 8½ cups/3½ pints/2 liters cold water
- 3 cups/14 oz/400 g garbanzo bean/chick pea flour
- salt to taste
- 5 tablespoons finely chopped parsley (optional)
- extra-virgin (or ordinary, good quality) olive oil for frying

Suggested wine: a dry red (Cerasuolo)

Pour about two-thirds of the water into a blender. Add the garbanzo bean flour and process, adding more water as necessary to form a lump-free pouring batter. ও Pour the mixture into a heavy-bottomed saucepan. Add salt to taste and bring slowly to a boil, stirring almost continuously. ও Continue cooking for about 30 minutes, stirring frequently, until it is very thick, soft, and smooth. Stir in the parsley, if using. ও Lightly oil a baking sheet or large shallow pan, and use a spatula to spread the mixture evenly to a thickness of about ¼ in/5 mm. ও Leave until completely cold, then cut into short strips or squares. ও Fry in batches in plenty of very hot oil until golden brown. ও Drain well and serve piping hot.

Reminiscent of the Ligurian recipe for fried Panissa *or* Paniccia, *this recipe comes from the capital of Sicily, Palermo, where the fritters are sprinkled with a few drops of lemon juice and often used as a filling for bread rolls.*

Capunata

Sweet and Sour Vegetable Appetizer

Serves 4–6

*Preparation: 1 hour + several hours'
     standing time*

Cooking: 50 minutes

Recipe grading: easy

- 2 lb/1 kg eggplants/aubergine, cut into ½ in/1 cm cubes
- coarse sea salt
- ⅔ cup/5 fl oz/150 ml extra-virgin olive oil
- 4 tender stalks celery, trimmed and cut into ¾ in/2 cm lengths
- 1 large onion, sliced
- 2 cups/1 lb/500 g sieved tomatoes
- 12 fresh basil leaves, torn
- 1 small, firm pear, peeled, cored, and diced (optional)
- 1½ tablespoons capers
- 20 green or black olives, pitted and chopped
- 2½ tablespoons pine nuts
- 2 tablespoons sugar
- scant ½ cup/3½ fl oz/100 ml Italian wine vinegar
- 2½ tablespoons coarsely chopped roasted almonds (or 3 tablespoons toasted breadcrumbs)

Suggested wine: a dry rosé (Sciacca)

Layer the eggplants in a colander, sprinkling with coarse salt and leave for at least 1 hour. Drain and dry on paper towels. ❧ Heat about two-thirds of the oil in a skillet and sauté the eggplant over a moderate heat for 10 minutes. Set aside. ❧ Blanch the celery in boiling salted water for 5 minutes. Drain and set aside. ❧ Sauté the onion in the remaining oil until pale golden brown and add the tomato and half the basil. Cook for 10 minutes and then add the celery, pear (if using), capers, olives, pine nuts, sugar, and vinegar. ❧ Continue simmering for 20 minutes, stirring now and then. ❧ Add the eggplant and the rest of the basil. Cook, stirring occasionally, for another 10 minutes. ❧ Remove from the heat and when the mixture is just warm, transfer to a serving dish, heaping it up into a mound. The eggplant should have absorbed most of the moisture. ❧ Leave to stand for several hours or overnight. ❧ Serve at room temperature, adding a few fresh basil leaves and sprinkling with the almonds or breadcrumbs. ❧ Capunata keeps well for 3–4 days if refrigerated in a tightly closed container.

*This recipe is part of Sicilian culinary history
and is still very popular. The subtle mixture of
sweet and sour flavors is present in many of
the island's dishes.*

Primi piatti

Il primo, or first course (actually served second, after the appetizer), plays an important role in a Sicilian meal. *Minestre,* or broth-based soups, often dating back hundreds of years, are a traditional part of formal Sicilian meals. But for everyday fare, pasta – prepared in countless different ways – is by far the most popular choice. Rice-based dishes, either baked in the oven or served as risotto, are also common. Both pasta and rice dishes use the most imaginative combinations of vegetables, fish, and cheese. The subtleties of their flavors and aromas are unique to Sicily.

Sciusceddu Pasquali

Easter Soup

Serves 4
Preparation: 10 minutes
Cooking: 7–8 minutes
Recipe grading: easy

Place the meat in a mixing bowl and add one egg, the grated cheese, garlic, parsley, nutmeg, and salt. ❧ Mix well and shape heaped teaspoonfuls into little meatballs. ❧ Bring the stock to a boil in a large saucepan. Drop in the meatballs and cook for 4–5 minutes. ❧ Beat the remaining eggs and combine with the ricotta, breadcrumbs, and raisins (if using), adding salt to taste, to make a smooth, creamy mixture. ❧ Pour the egg mixture into the hot stock and stir with a fork for about 1 minute, until the egg sets into tiny shreds. ❧ Serve immediately.

- 2½ cups/8 oz/250 g ground lean beef or pork
- 3 eggs
- 2½ tablespoons freshly grated pecorino cheese
- ½ clove garlic, finely chopped
- 1 tablespoon finely chopped parsley
- freshly grated nutmeg
- salt to taste
- 4¼ cups/1¾ pints/1 liter meat stock (homemade or bouillon cube)
- 1 cup/8 oz/250 g soft fresh ricotta cheese
- 2½ tablespoons fine, dry breadcrumbs
- 1 tablespoon seedless white raisins/sultanas (optional)

Suggested wine: a young dry white (Bianco di Donnafugata)

Sicilian soups are usually thick and hearty, made with vegetables, rice or pasta. This is one of the island's few light, stock-based soups, and it comes from Messina.

Pasta a la Norma
Pasta with Ricotta and Eggplant

Slice the eggplants quite thinly lengthwise. Place them in layers in a colander and sprinkle each layer with salt. Leave to stand for at least 1 hour, then rinse thoroughly and dry on paper towels. ❧ Use a fork to break the salted ricotta into fairly small, crumbly pieces (or chop the pecorino into small pieces with a knife). ❧ Place the tomatoes in a large, heavy-bottomed saucepan with the garlic and oil and simmer for 30 minutes, stirring occasionally. ❧ Sieve the thick tomato sauce (or process in a blender) and return to the pan to keep hot over a very low heat. ❧ Bring plenty of salted water to a boil and add the spaghetti. ❧ Fry the eggplant slices in hot oil and drain on paper towels when browned on both sides. ❧ Drain the spaghetti when cooked *al dente*. Transfer to a serving bowl. Add the tomato sauce and mix in just over half the cheese and the basil. ❧ Serve immediately, topping each portion with eggplant slices and the remaining ricotta or pecorino.

Serves 4

Preparation: 15 minutes + 1 hour's standing

Cooking: 35 minutes

Recipe grading: fairly easy

- 3 medium eggplants/aubergines, long not round
- coarse sea salt
- 5 oz/150 g salted ricotta cheese or semi-hard pecorino cheese
- 1¼ lb/625 g fresh or canned tomatoes, skinned and chopped
- 1 clove garlic, crushed
- 6 tablespoons extra-virgin olive oil
- 14 oz/400 g spaghetti
- extra-virgin (or ordinary, good quality) olive oil for frying
- 8 fresh basil leaves, torn
- freshly ground black pepper

Suggested wine: a young rosé (Etna rosato)

This recipe comes from Catania and is named after Bellini's masterpiece, the opera Norma. *The sauce is equally good with a number of other types of pasta, such as penne or cavateddi.*

Serves 4
Preparation: 10 minutes
Cooking: 50 minutes
Recipe grading: easy

- 1½ cups/5 oz/150 g ground lean pork
- 1½ cups/5 oz/150 g ground lean veal
- 4 tablespoons extra-virgin olive oil
- 1 tablespoon tomato paste
- scant ½ cup/3½ fl oz/100 ml dry white or dry red wine
- 1 cup/8 oz/250 g canned tomatoes
- salt to taste
- freshly ground black pepper
- 14 oz/400 g pappardelle (wide tagliatelle or ribbon noodles)
- 2½ oz/75 g salted ricotta cheese
- 7 oz/200 g fresh ricotta cheese
- ½ cup/2 oz/60 g freshly grated pecorino cheese

Suggested wine: a full-bodied white
(Partinico)

Lasagni a Palermitana
Pappardelle Palermo-Style

In a fairly large, heavy-bottomed saucepan, sauté the meat in the oil over a moderate heat, using a fork to break up any lumps. ❧ When the meat is lightly browned, add the tomato paste mixed with the wine. Cook for 4–5 minutes, then add the tomatoes with salt and pepper to taste. Simmer over a low heat for 40 minutes. ❧ Bring plenty of salted water to a boil and add the pappardelle. ❧ While the pasta is cooking, use a fork to break the salted ricotta into fairly small, crumbly pieces. ❧ When the pasta is nearly done, mix the fresh ricotta with 2 tablespoons of the cooking water in a large, heated serving dish. ❧ Drain the pasta and toss with the fresh ricotta and meat sauce. ❧ Sprinkle with the salted ricotta and pecorino cheese and serve.

In Palermo this dish is traditionally served at New Year's.

Maccu di Favi

Fava Bean Soup

Bring the water to a boil in a heavy-bottomed saucepan and add the beans. Partially cover, and simmer for about 3 hours over a low heat, stirring from time to time. Add the fennel and the chili pepper after 1½ hours. ❧ After 2 hours, stir more frequently, crushing the beans as much as possible with a large wooden spoon. They should gradually turn into a coarse purée. Add a little boiling water if the soup becomes too thick. ❧ Season with salt only when the beans are cooked. ❧ Place the toasted bread in heated soup bowls and drizzle with a little oil. Ladle the soup over the bread, drizzle with the remaining oil, and serve piping hot.

Serves 4

Preparation: 8–10 hours for soaking the beans

Cooking: 3 hours

Recipe grading: easy

- 5¼ cups/2 generous pints/1.25 liters water
- 1½ cups/10 oz/300 g dried fava beans/broad beans, soaked for 8-10 hours, drained and well rinsed
- small bunch of wild fennel, coarsely chopped
- ½ chili pepper, whole or crumbled, seeded
- salt to taste
- 4 slices of 2–3-day-old coarse white bread, toasted
- 4 tablespoons extra-virgin olive oil

Suggested wine: a dry rosé
(Fontanarossa di Cerda)

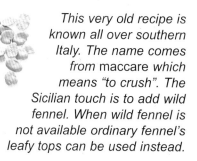

This very old recipe is known all over southern Italy. The name comes from maccare which means "to crush". The Sicilian touch is to add wild fennel. When wild fennel is not available ordinary fennel's leafy tops can be used instead.

Risu a Palermitana
Palermo-Style Risotto

Serves 4–6

Preparation: 20 minutes + 1 hour's standing

Cooking: 40 minutes

Recipe grading: fairly easy

- 2 large eggplants/aubergines
- coarse sea salt
- 1 medium onion, thinly sliced
- 8 tablespoons extra-virgin olive oil
- 1½ tablespoons finely chopped parsley
- 4–5 fresh basil leaves, torn
- 1 lb/500 g fresh or canned tomatoes, skinned and coarsely chopped
- salt to taste
- freshly ground black pepper
- 2 tablespoons onion, finely chopped
- 2 cups/14 oz/400 g Italian Arborio rice
- 3½ cups/1½ pints/800 ml stock (homemade or bouillon cube), boiling
- 1 cup/4 oz/125 g freshly grated caciocavallo cheese
- a little all-purpose/plain white flour
- extra-virgin (or ordinary, good quality) olive oil for frying
- 10 fresh basil leaves

Suggested wine: a young dry rosé (Etna rosato)

This layered dish looks very impressive. The recipe will yield 4 ample servings if served as a main course or 6 generous helpings as a first course.

Slice the eggplants thinly lengthwise and place them in a colander, sprinkling each layer with salt. Leave to stand for at least 1 hour, then rinse thoroughly and dry on paper towels. ❧ In a heavy-bottomed saucepan, sauté the onion in half the oil for 2–3 minutes, then add the parsley, basil, tomatoes, salt, and pepper. ❧ Simmer over low heat for 20–25 minutes, then set aside. ❧ For the risotto, use a heavy-bottomed casserole and sauté the chopped onion in the oil. When it starts to color, add the rice and stir for 2 minutes to coat the grains with oil. ❧ Add about half a cup of stock and cook over a higher heat, stirring frequently and moistening with stock when necessary. ❧ When it is cooked *al dente*, turn off the heat and stir in 2½ tablespoons of the cheese. ❧ Meanwhile, coat the eggplants lightly with flour and fry in hot oil until they are golden brown on both sides. Remove from the pan and drain. ❧ Line the bottom of an oiled casserole with one-third of the eggplant and cover with half the risotto, half the remaining cheese, and almost half the sauce. Sprinkle the basil over the sauce and cover with half the remaining eggplant and the remaining rice, sauce, and basil. Top with eggplant and cheese. ❧ Bake in a preheated oven at 425°F/220°C/gas 7 for 10 minutes. Serve very hot.

Tomatoes: a Gift from America

Spanish explorers brought the tomato back to Europe from South America, probably around the middle of the 16th century. For a long time it was regarded as a botanical curiosity and serious doubts were entertained as to whether it really was edible. Only in the early 19th century did people realize how delicious and versatile it was; from then on it played an increasingly important role in cuisine, and was instrumental in changing Mediterranean cooking into its modern form. Other parts of the world also made these American newcomers very welcome and it is difficult to imagine what modern cooking would be like without them.

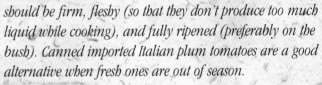

Italians make sauces using fleshy, ripe plum tomatoes. If you can't get the plum tomatoes, choose another variety with the same characteristics: they should be firm, fleshy (so that they don't produce too much liquid while cooking), and fully ripened (preferably on the bush). Canned imported Italian plum tomatoes are a good alternative when fresh ones are out of season.

There are many variations in method and cooking times when making Sicilian homemade tomato sauce, but the basic ingredients are the same: tomatoes, onions, garlic, basil, oil, salt and freshly ground black pepper. The only hard and fast rule is always to use the finest ingredients.

Capuliatu (meaning "chopped") is a Sicilian specialty. It is similar to dried tomatoes and is often used instead of strattu (Sicilian tomato paste) or served as a spread on sliced bread. It is made by finely chopping sun-dried tomatoes with plenty of fresh basil leaves, chili peppers, and a few bay leaves. The mixture is preserved in oil and stored in glass jars.

BASIC TOMATO SAUCE

For four, to serve with pasta or meat

2 cloves garlic, finely chopped
4 tablespoons extra-virgin olive oil
1 lb/500 g fresh or canned tomatoes, skinned and coarsely chopped
6–8 fresh basil leaves, torn

In a heavy-bottomed pan, sauté the garlic in the oil briefly (don't let the garlic turn brown or it will give your sauce a bitter flavor). ❧ Add the tomatoes and season with salt and pepper. Simmer over a low heat for about 30 minutes, or until the sauce has reduced to the required density. Never cover the sauce with a lid; the tomatoes need to evaporate their liquid gently. If covered, they will lose their fresh tomato taste. ❧ Turn off the heat, stir in the basil, and serve. ❧ For a tastier sauce, sauté 1 tablespoon of finely chopped parsley and/or 1 finely chopped medium onion with the garlic before adding the tomatoes. ❧ For a spicy sauce, add chili peppers to taste. ❧ This sauce will keep in the refrigerator for several days and also freezes very well.

The strong Sicilian sunshine is ideal for drying tomatoes. Fresh tomatoes are sliced in half, sprinkled with salt and left in the sun to dry for several days. They are then preserved in oil with basil, bay leaves, and chili peppers. They can be served as an appetizer or snack, but are also added to many dishes to give a fuller, more intense flavor.

Sicilians make a very special tomato paste, called strattu *or* astrattu *which makes industrially produced tomato paste seem tasteless in comparison. The only ingredients and processes used are tomatoes, the sun, special sieves to get rid of the skins and seeds, prolonged, gentle cooking, and large tables on which the thick sieved tomato is spread out to dry. The process is extremely labor-intensive: the tomato purée has to be patiently stirred time after time to ensure that it dries evenly in the sun without forming a hard crust on top. The resulting paste is a wonderful deep red color. It is stored in earthenware pots or glass jars, the surface covered with a film of olive oil, and keeps well for many months. Strattu is a vital ingredient in many vegetable soups, sauces, liquids used for braising meat, sweet-sour recipes, and many other dishes.*

Risu a Siciliana
Sicilian Rice

Serves 4
Preparation: 15 minutes
Cooking: 20 minutes
Recipe grading: easy

- 1³/₄ cups/12 oz/350 g Italian Arborio rice
- salt to taste
- ¹/₂ medium onion, thinly sliced
- 4 tablespoons extra-virgin olive oil
- 1 salted anchovy (rinsed and boned) or 2 anchovy fillets
- scant ¹/₂ cup/3¹/₂ fl oz/100 ml dry white wine
- 1 tablespoon Italian red or white wine vinegar
- 4–5 fresh or canned tomatoes, skinned and coarsely chopped
- juice of 2 lemons
- ¹/₂ chili pepper, seeded and crumbled
- 1 teaspoon finely chopped fresh marjoram
- 3–4 fresh basil leaves
- 8 large, fleshy black olives, pitted and cut into quarters

Suggested wine: a young dry rosé (Etna rosato)

The various, very different, flavors in this dish go extremely well together and the sauce is the perfect accompaniment to rice.

Bring plenty of salted water to a boil in a large saucepan. Add the rice and cook for 16–18 minutes or until just tender. ❧ While it is cooking, sauté the onion in oil and then add the anchovies, crushing them with a fork. ❧ Add the wine and vinegar and cook, uncovered, until the liquid has evaporated. ❧ Add the tomatoes, lemon juice, chili, marjoram, basil, and olives, and simmer over moderate heat for 7–8 minutes, stirring now and then. ❧ Drain the rice and transfer to a heated serving dish. Pour the sauce over the top. ❧ Serve at once.

Risu che Caciuocculi e Piseddi

Rice with Artichokes and Peas

Serves 4
Preparation: 10 minutes
Cooking: 25–30 minutes
Recipe grading: easy

Strip off the outer leaves of the artichokes and cut off the top third of the leaves. Remove the "choke" and peel the remaining stalk, rubbing all the cut surfaces with lemon juice to prevent discoloration. Cut into quarters lengthwise. ☞ If using defrosted artichoke hearts, cut them in halves or quarters. ☞ Sauté the onion in the oil. Add the garlic, cook for 1 minute and then add the anchovies, crushing them with a fork so that they dissolve in the oil. ☞ Add the artichokes and peas. Season with salt and pepper and moisten with the first measure of water. Cover and cook until it has evaporated. ☞ Add the rice and stir for 1 minute, then add the boiling water and continue to cook, stirring frequently, and adding more water as necessary. ☞ When the rice is cooked *al dente*, serve at once, sprinkled with the cheese.

- 4–5 baby artichokes or 12–16 defrosted frozen artichoke hearts
- 1 lemon
- 1 medium onion, thinly sliced
- 4 tablespoons extra-virgin olive oil
- 1–2 cloves garlic, finely chopped
- 2 salted anchovies (rinsed and boned) or 4 anchovy fillets
- 1 cup/5 oz/150 g peas, fresh or frozen
- salt to taste
- freshly ground black pepper
- about 1/4 cup/2 fl oz/60 ml water
- 1 3/4 cups/12 oz/350 g Italian Arborio rice
- about 4 tablespoons boiling water
  - 1/2 cup/2 oz/60 g freshly grated caciocavallo (or pecorino) cheese

Suggested wine: a young dry white
(Bianco di Donnafugata)

Serves 4

Preparation: 30 minutes

Cooking: 50 minutes

Recipe grading: complicated

- 3 quarts/5 pints/3 liters water
- 1 tablespoon salt
- 7 oz/200 g wild fennel
- 12 oz/350 g fresh or defrosted frozen sardines
- 1 medium onion, finely chopped
- 6 tablespoons extra-virgin olive oil
- 2–3 salted anchovies (rinsed and boned) or 4–6 anchovy fillets
- 2 tablespoons small, seedless white raisins/sultanas
- 2½ tablespoons pine nuts
- ¼ cup/1½ oz/45 g toasted almonds, chopped
- freshly ground black pepper
- ¼ teaspoon saffron, dissolved in 1½ tablespoons hot water
- 10 oz/300 g long pasta (bucatini, perciatelli or mezzi ziti)
- ⅔ cup/2 oz/60 g fine breadcrumbs, toasted

Suggested wine: a full-bodied white (Partinico)

Pasta che Sardi
Pasta with Sardines

Bring the water to a boil in a very large saucepan and add the salt and fennel. Simmer for 15 minutes, then drain, reserving the water to cook the pasta. ❧ Squeeze the fennel to remove excess moisture and chop coarsely. ❧ Remove any scales from the sardines and gently pull off their heads (the viscera will come away with the heads). Use kitchen scissors to cut down their bellies and lay them out flat. ❧ Sauté the onion in the oil, then add the anchovies, crushing them with a fork so that they dissolve in the oil. ❧ Add the sardines, raisins, pine nuts, and almonds, and season with salt and pepper. ❧ Cook over a moderate heat for 10 minutes before adding the fennel and saffron. Stir gently to avoid breaking up the fish. Reduce the heat, cover and simmer for another 10 minutes. ❧ Bring the fennel-flavored water to a boil, add the pasta, and cook until *al dente*. Drain and mix carefully with the sardines and sauce. ❧ Transfer to an oiled, heated ovenproof dish and sprinkle the breadcrumbs over the top. ❧ Bake in a preheated oven at 425°F/220°C/gas 7 for 6–10 minutes. ❧ Serve immediately.

This recipe comes from Palermo but it has become such a favorite with the inhabitants of the whole island that it is now regarded as typical Sicilian food.

Cheese

The combination of Sicily's warm, Mediterranean climate, its special vegetation, and a centuries-old tradition in cheese-making, makes for some stunningly distinctive flavors and aromas in the local cheeses. Three main types of cheese are produced on the island: *Pecorino, Ragusano,* and *Ricotta.* However, depending on how they are treated and aged, they each produce several different varieties of cheese.

The fresh curd is placed in wicker molds which leave their characteristic marks on the cheese as it drains and becomes firmer. If eaten within a few days, this unsalted curd is called Tuma *and it has a very mild, bland flavor.*

Sicilian pecorino cheese is made with ewe's milk. It is well known in Italy as a high quality cheese and there are strict regulations governing how and where it is made. Its origins go back to ancient times and the Greeks knew and prized it. Depending on how long it is aged, its taste and texture change, as does its name.

After the first dry-salting of the cheese's surface it is called Primo sale *(first salting). Still a soft cheese, it has more flavor and makes a delicious table cheese.*

After further aging and salting it acquires a stronger flavor, progressing from a semi-hard sliceable cheese to a hard cheese, suitable for serving at table or for grating.

But the possibilities of Pecorino *do not stop there: if a generous sprinkling of whole black peppercorns are added to the curd, this produces a spicy cheese called* Piacintinu. *In the area surrounding Enna in central Sicily, saffron is also added, giving the cheese a wonderful sunny color and extra flavor. The curd is left to drain and shape in wicker molds or in larger cheese forms and, depending on the length of time it is left to mature, it becomes a semi-hard, sliceable cheese or a hard, grating cheese. Both types are excellent.*

Ragusano *cheese (a type of* caciocavallo, *also made in other parts of Italy) is made from full cream cow's milk, occasionally mixed with ewe's milk. The origin of the name* Caciocavallo *has been the subject of much controversy but the most convincing explanation is that it comes from* cacio a cavallo *(literally, "cheese on a horse") which describes the way the cheese is aged. Pairs of cheeses weighing anything from 13 to 27 lb /6 to12 kg are tied together with string (which marks the surface of the cheese), and slung over a pole so that they dangle like a rider's legs. Caciocavallo is eaten at various stages of maturity. When young it has a delicate taste, but as it ages this gradually becomes stronger and fuller. Provolone cheese can be substituted if caciocavallo is unobtainable.*

Ricotta *cheese is made all over Italy. Traditionally it was made with ewe's milk although it is now usually made with mixed ewe's and cow's milk or just cow's milk. Do try pure ewe's milk ricotta if you can get it; it has very distinctive flavor. In Sicily fresh ricotta with no salt added is mainly used for patisserie and desserts. When very fresh it is also delicious just by itself or mixed with a few drops of vanilla extract (essence) and a little sugar. Ricotta salata (salted ricotta), which keeps better, is used in a variety of dishes. It is sometimes baked briefly in a very hot oven, so that its surface turns a deep gold while it remains snowy white inside. Ricotta salata can also be aged to be used as a grating cheese. Ricotta sicca (dry ricotta) is lightly salted and left to dry in the sun. When hard it can be grated, or used in cooking by removing little curly strips by running the prongs of a fork down the outer surface while pressing firmly.*

Pasta che' Vruocculi

Pasta with Cauliflower

Serves 4
Preparation: 15 minutes
Cooking: 40 minutes
Recipe grading: easy

- 1 small cauliflower
- salt to taste
- 12 oz/350 g pasta (bucatini, mezzi ziti)
- 1 medium onion, thinly sliced
- 6 tablespoons extra–virgin olive oil
- 2 salted anchovies (rinsed and boned) or 4 anchovy fillets
- 2½ tablespoons small seedless white raisins/sultanas
- 2½ tablespoons pine nuts
- ¼ teaspoon saffron, dissolved in 3 tablespoons hot water
- freshly ground black pepper
- ½ cup/2 oz/60 g freshly grated pecorino cheese (optional)

Suggested wine: a dry white (Alcamo)

Boil the cauliflower in plenty of salted water until it is just tender. Drain, reserving the water. Divide the cauliflower into small florets. ❧ Bring the water back to a boil and add the pasta. ❧ Meanwhile, sauté the onion for 1–2 minutes in the oil in a large, heavy-bottomed saucepan. Add the anchovies, raisins, pine nuts, and saffron. Stir for 2–3 minutes, then add the cauliflower and continue cooking over a very low heat, stirring occasionally. ❧ When the pasta is cooked *al dente*, drain and add to the cauliflower mixture. ❧ Combine carefully, then transfer to a heated serving dish and sprinkle generously with pepper. ❧ Serve hot. ❧ For a hearty winter dish, transfer the pasta and cauliflower mixture to a heated ovenproof dish and sprinkle with the pecorino cheese. Place in a preheated oven at 425°F/220°C /gas 7 for 10 minutes, or until the cheese topping has turned golden brown.

This pasta dish is a great favorite all over Sicily. There are several versions; this one comes from Palermo.

Tagghiarini che Caciuocculi

Tagliolini with Artichokes

Serves 4
Preparation: 15 minutes
Cooking: 30 minutes
Recipe grading: easy

Prepare the artichokes as described on page 37, cutting them lengthwise into thin slices. ❧ Sauté the onion in the oil in a flameproof casserole until it is tender but not browned. ❧ Add the artichokes and season with salt and pepper. Stir over a moderate heat for 2–3 minutes. ❧ Pour in the water, cover and cook for about 20 minutes, or until very tender but not mushy. ❧ Cook the tagliolini in plenty of boiling salted water until they are cooked *al dente.* ❧ Break the eggs into a deep, heated serving dish, beat with a fork and add about 5 tablespoons of the cheese. ❧ Drain the pasta and mix with the egg mixture, then stir in the artichokes. ❧ Sprinkle with the remaining cheese and serve at once.

- 8 very fresh baby artichokes or 16 fresh or defrosted frozen artichoke hearts
- 2½ tablespoons finely chopped onion
- 5 tablespoons extra-virgin olive oil
- salt to taste
- freshly ground black pepper
- ½ cup/4 fl oz/125 ml water
- 14 oz/400 g tagliolini (thin ribbon noodles)
- 3–4 very fresh large eggs
- 7 tablespoons freshly grated pecorino cheese

Suggested wine: a young dry white (Bianco di Donnafugata)

This unusual recipe comes from the Enna region. The addition of eggs to the artichoke mixture results in a rich and creamy sauce.

Pasta ca Muddica
Pasta with Toasted Breadcrumbs

Serves 4
Preparation: 10 minutes
Cooking: 15–20 minutes
Recipe grading: easy

- 2 whole cloves garlic, slightly crushed
- scant ½ cup/3½ fl oz/100 ml extra-virgin olive oil
- 5–6 salted anchovies (rinsed and boned) or about 10 anchovy fillets
- 1 tablespoon finely chopped parsley
- 1 lb/500 g fresh or canned tomatoes, skinned and coarsely chopped
- 14 oz/400 g spaghetti or small macaroni (maccheroncini)
- salt to taste
- 4 tablespoons fine dry breadcrumbs, toasted

Suggested wine: a dry white
(Alcamo)

Sauté the garlic in the oil in a large, heavy-bottomed saucepan until it starts to color, then remove and discard. ❧ Add the anchovies, crushing them with a fork so that they dissolve in the flavored oil. ❧ Add the parsley and the tomatoes, but no salt. Simmer over a low heat for 15–20 minutes. ❧ Cook the pasta in plenty of boiling salted water until *al dente*. Drain, add to the sauce and toss briefly. ❧ Transfer to a heated serving dish. Sprinkle with the toasted breadcrumbs and serve hot.

This simple dish is traditionally served during Lent. There are many versions from the various regions of Sicily.

Pasta cu l'Aulivi
Pasta with Olives

Serves 4
Preparation: 10 minutes
Cooking: 20 minutes
Recipe grading: easy

Place the tomatoes in a heavy-bottomed saucepan. Add the garlic and simmer over a low heat for 15 minutes. ❧ Add the oil, olives, oregano, and chili pepper and cook for 2 minutes more. Season with salt. ❧ Cook the spaghetti in plenty of boiling salted water until *al dente*. ❧ Drain and add to the tomato mixture. Toss briefly and serve. Cheese is not served with this dish.

- 1 lb/500 g fresh or canned tomatoes, skinned and coarsely chopped
- 2 cloves garlic, finely chopped
- 5 tablespoons extra-virgin olive oil
- 1¼ cups/6 oz/180 g black olives, pitted and coarsely chopped
- 2 teaspoons oregano
- ½ chili pepper, seeded and crumbled
- salt to taste
- 14 oz/400 g spaghetti (or bucatini)

Suggested wine: a dry red (Cerasuolo)

Olives, eggplant, and artichokes are among the most typical ingredients of many Sicilian recipes.

Pizze e pane

There are many different types of pizza and bread in traditional Sicilian cuisine. Generally speaking, Sicilian pizzas have much thicker and softer bases than pizzas from other regions of Italy. Stuffed focaccias, called *scacce* in Sicilian dialect, and country-style pies made with bread dough, known as *mpanate*, are also popular and widespread. A wide variety of fillings are used to stuff the focaccias and pies, although they all reflect traditional Sicilian flavors. Many of the country-style pies contain meat or fish, and are often quite elaborate.

Pasta da Pane
Basic Bread and Pizza Dough

Serves 2–4

Preparation: 20 minutes + 1 hour's rising

Cooking: none

Recipe grading: fairly easy

Crumble the yeast into a small bowl and add the sugar and half the water, stirring until the yeast dissolves. ❧ Leave to stand for 10 minutes in a warm (not hot) place; the surface will become frothy. ❧ Sift the flour into a large mixing bowl with the salt. Make a well in the center and pour in the yeast liquid, the oil, and most of the remaining water. ❧ Stir with a wooden spoon until the flour has been absorbed. Add a little more warm water if necessary. ❧ Place the dough on a floured work surface and knead until it becomes very soft and elastic. ❧ Shape into a ball and place in a large bowl. Cover with a large clean cloth folded in half and leave to rise in a warm place, away from drafts, for 1 hour or until the dough has doubled in volume. ❧ Knead the dough briefly on a lightly floured surface just before using.

- 1 tablespoon/¹⁄₂ oz/15 g fresh compressed/baker's yeast or 1¹⁄₂ packets active dried yeast
- 1 teaspoon sugar
- about ³⁄₄ cup/6 fl oz/180 ml lukewarm water
- 3 cups/12 oz/350 g unbleached or all-purpose/strong or plain flour + 2 tablespoons extra flour
- 1–2 teaspoons salt (to taste)
- 2¹⁄₂ tablespoons extra virgin olive oil

Use this basic bread dough for all the recipes in this section. If ingredients vary, this is noted in the recipe. It is difficult to give an exact amount of water as flour varies so much in absorbency. The quantities given should yield about 1¹⁄₄ lb/ 625 g of dough, enough for a pizza with a diameter of 10-11 in/25-28 cm.

Serves 2–4

Preparation: 25 minutes + 1 hour's rising

Cooking: 25–30 minutes

Recipe grading: fairly easy

- 1 quantity basic dough (see recipe, page 49)
- salt to taste
- freshly ground black pepper
- 5 tablespoons extra-virgin olive oil
- 2 tender, young globe artichokes, trimmed and thinly sliced
- 1 cup/8 oz/250 g coarsely crumbled or grated salted ricotta cheese
- 4–6 anchovy fillets, coarsely chopped

Suggested wine: a young dry white (Bianco di Donnafugata)

Pizza ai Carciofi
Pizza with Artichoke Topping

Roll out the dough so that it will fit into a 10–11 in/25–28 cm pizza pan or layer cake pan which has been greased with olive oil. ❧ Press the surface of the dough with your fingertips to make little dimples in it. ❧ Sprinkle with salt and pepper. Drizzle with 2½ tablespoons of the oil, then spread the artichoke slices out in a single layer. ❧ Distribute the cheese and anchovy fillets on top. ❧ Bake in a preheated oven at 425°F/220°C/gas 7 for 25–30 minutes. ❧ Only the youngest artichoke hearts, without any choke are used in the traditional recipe. If you can't get them, use 6–8 thinly sliced fresh or defrosted frozen artichoke hearts.

This recipe comes from Enna, in the very heart of Sicily.

Festivals and Feast Days

Colorfully decorated horses pulling carts painted with scenes showing combat between Christian knights and Saracens are typical of feast days in the provinces of Catania and Palermo.

Every town and village in Sicily, no matter how small, celebrates its patron saint's day and religious holidays with special festivities and most also have other feast days to commemorate important events in local history. Joyous open-air feasting in village streets, solemn processions and pilgrimages, public acts of worship and penitence, colorful parades, fireworks and family gatherings are familiar sights in the various parts of Sicily throughout the year.

The regional capital of Palermo celebrates its patron saint, Santa Rosalia, with seven days of feasting known as *'U festinu* (the festival). According to the legend the Saint died after twelve years living in a cave as a hermit on September 4, 1160. Nearly 500 years later, in 1624, Palermo was struck by a terrible plague which threatened the very life of the city. Some time beforehand the Saint had appeared to a local shepherd who was lost in a storm, admonishing him to tell the Bishop of Palermo where her bones could be found. She also predicted that the shepherd would die of plague. As he lay dying, the man told the whereabouts of the Saint's bones. The Bishop was alerted and the bones carried in solemn procession through the streets of the suffering city; as they passed the plague abated. This occurred on July 15 and ever since then seven days of feasting have been held in her honor.

Pupi co l'ova (Bread with eggs) consist of plain bread dough intricately shaped and wrapped around hard-cooked (hard-boiled) eggs, which sometimes have had their shells painted in various colors. These are an indispensable part of Easter festivities all over the island, although their name changes from place to place.

Cuddura, Cudduredda or Cudduruni, a word derived from the Greek kuddura to describe a type of focaccia, are flat breads imaginatively shaped as flowers, dolls, and animals. Sometimes eggs are added to the dough to make it richer.

In Sicily, where a strong religious sense has survived longer than in many other parts of Europe, there are literally hundreds of different types and shapes of bread and many of the more intriguingly shaped ones are linked to various festivals of the Christian year. Saint Blaise, who is said to protect people against sore throats, has a type of bread called cannarozza *dedicated to him, shaped to represent the trachea. Minnuzza, a bread from Ucria, is rounded and fashioned to look like a breast in honor of Saint Agatha: women who lacked milk to feed their babies or who were suffering from pains or maladies of the breast prayed to her for help. Saint Lucy, the patron saint of sight, whose feast day falls on December 13, is commemorated by a special loaf with two narrow strips of dough twisted around the loaf in opposite directions, meeting in the center to form a stylized representation of a person's eyes.*

Sfinciuni

Pizza with Mixed Topping

Roll out the dough so that it fits into a 10–11 in/25–28 cm diameter oiled pizza pan or layer cake pan. ❧ Press the surface of the dough with your fingertips to make little dimples in it. ❧ Sprinkle with a little salt and 2½ tablespoons of the oil. Top with the ingredients in the following order: onion, anchovies, cheese, olives, tomatoes (if using), and oregano. Drizzle with the remaining oil. ❧ Bake in a preheated oven at 425°F/220°C/gas 7 for 20–25 minutes. ❧ Serve hot or at room temperature.

Serves 4–6

Preparation: 25 minutes + 1 hour's rising

Cooking: 20–25 minutes

Recipe grading: fairly easy

- 1 quantity basic dough (see recipe, page 49)
- salt to taste
- 5 tablespoons extra-virgin olive oil
- 1 medium onion, thinly sliced
- 10–12 anchovy fillets, very coarsely chopped or torn into small pieces
- 5 oz/150 g caciocavallo or semi-mature pecorino cheese, thinly sliced
- 10 black olives, pitted and coarsely chopped
- 2 large tomatoes, skinned and diced (optional)
- 1 teaspoon oregano

Suggested wine: a dry red (Rosso di Donnafugata)

"Sfinciuni" is a Sicilian word for a wide variety of dough-based preparations, including pancakes, focaccias, pizzas, and various savory and sweet pies which are fried or baked in the oven. Anchovies are a vital ingredient in this and many other typical Sicilian dishes.

Pizza di Indivia Riccia

Pizza with Chicory Topping

Serves 4–6

Preparation: 25 minutes + 1 hour's rising

Cooking: 25 minutes

Recipe grading: fairly easy

- 1 quantity basic dough (see recipe, page 49)
- salt to taste
- 5 tablespoons extra-virgin olive oil
- 4–5 firm, ripe tomatoes, skinned and chopped
- 1 head chicory/curly endive
- 8 oz/250 g semi-hard, spicy provolone cheese, cubed
- 4 anchovy fillets, coarsely chopped (optional)
- 12 capers (optional)

Suggested wine: a dry red (Rosso di Donnafugata)

Roll out the dough so that it fits into a 10–11 in/25–28 cm oiled pizza pan or layer cake pan. ❧ Press the surface of the dough with your fingertips to make little dimples in it. ❧ Sprinkle with salt, drizzle with 2 tablespoons of oil, and scatter with the tomato. ❧ Bake in a preheated oven at 425°F/220°C/gas 7 for 15 minutes. ❧ While the pizza is cooking, rinse the chicory thoroughly. Discard the tougher, outer leaves, drain the inner leaves well and chop them coarsely. ❧ Take the pizza out of the oven, spread the chicory over it, and scatter with the cheese, anchovy, and capers (if using). ❧ Return the pizza to the oven for another 10 minutes. ❧ The chicory will wilt and discolor a little but will still be quite crunchy, contrasting pleasantly with the melted cheese.

This recipe comes from Messina.

Scaccia di Ricotta

Focaccia with Ricotta Stuffing

Divide the dough into 4 portions and roll each one into a rectangular sheet just under ¼ in/5 mm thick. ❧ Spread a quarter of the ricotta over one half of each rectangle, leaving a narrow border around the edge. ❧ Place a quarter of the sausage meat on top of the ricotta and sprinkle with a little pepper, salt, and oil. ❧ Fold the uncovered half of each rectangle over the filling and pinch the edges together, then fold them back over to form a narrow rolled edge. This will prevent any filling leaking out. ❧ Bake in a preheated oven at 425°F/220°C/gas 7 for 20 minutes, or until golden brown.

Serves 4–6

Preparation: 25 minutes + 1 hour's rising

Cooking: 20 minutes

Recipe grading: fairly easy

- 1 quantity basic dough (see recipe, page 49)
- 1¼ lb/625 g ricotta cheese
- about 2½ cups/12 oz/350 g fresh, spicy Italian sausage meat
- 3 tablespoons extra-virgin olive oil
- salt to taste
- freshly ground black pepper

Suggested wine: a dry red (Rosso di Donnafugata)

This stuffing comes from Ragusa, but there are many alternatives. Try sliced mild onions sautéed in oil with chopped, fresh tomatoes. Alternatively, stuff with diced fresh tomatoes, fresh basil leaves, slices of caciocavallo cheese, and a little fried, diced eggplant.

Serves 4–6
Preparation: 1 hour + 1 hour's rising
Cooking: 30–35 minutes
Recipe grading: fairly easy

- 1 quantity basic dough (see recipe, page 49), made with double the amount of olive oil
- 2 lb/1 kg spinach (uncooked weight), trimmed, washed, and cooked
- 1 medium cauliflower, trimmed, cut into small florets, and cooked
- ½ cup/4 fl oz/125 ml extra-virgin olive oil
- 7oz/200 g semi-mature spicy provolone cheese, diced
- 6 oz/180 g canned tuna in oil, drained and flaked
- 12 black olives, pitted and coarsely chopped

Suggested wine: a dry white (Alcamo)

'Mpanata di Agrigento
Agrigento-Style Country Pie

Prepare the dough. ꙮ Drain the cooked spinach well and squeeze out excess moisture. ꙮ Sauté the spinach and cauliflower in 2 tablespoons of the oil. ꙮ Grease a cake pan at least 2½ in/6 cm deep, and measuring 9½ in/24 cm in diameter. ꙮ When the dough has risen, divide it into two unequal parts (about two-thirds/one-third) and roll out the larger piece into a disk ⅛ in/3 mm thick to line the bottom and sides of the cake pan, slightly overlapping the edge. ꙮ Spread with the spinach and cover with the cauliflower, cheese, tuna, and olives. ꙮ Roll out the smaller piece of dough to the same thickness and slightly larger than the diameter of the pan. ꙮ Place on top of the filling. Pinch the edges together, then fold them over toward the center and tuck under to make a neat rolled edge. ꙮ Brush the surface with the remaining oil and prick with a fork. ꙮ Bake in a preheated oven at 400°F/200°C/gas 6 for 30–35 minutes or until the crust is golden brown. ꙮ Serve very hot.

This hearty savory pie comes from Agrigento, which is also famous for the spectacular ancient ruins still standing in the Valley of the Temples.

Secondi piatti

Beef cattle are now reared in Sicily, but until recently only working animals past their prime were slaughtered for meat, which was tough and dry. This is why many traditional recipes use ground meat to make meatballs or rissoles. Sheep and goat meat are more typical. Lamb and kid, traditionally served at Easter, are now eaten throughout the year. The sweet and sour flavors in some recipes show the influence of Arabian cooking. Fresh fish and seafood have always been served. More surprising are the recipes of Northern European origin for preserved fish, such as salt cod and stockfish, which found their way into Sicilian cooking at a very early date.

Agneddu Agglassatu

Braised Lamb

Sauté the scallions or onion briefly in the oil over a very low heat in a large flameproof casserole. ❧ Add the pork fat and stir until it has melted. Add the lamb and brown all over. ❧ Pour in the wine and cook, uncovered, over a moderate heat until it has evaporated. ❧ Stir in the parsley, garlic, salt, and pepper and then add most of the stock. Cover and cook over a low heat for 45 minutes. ❧ Add the potatoes and more stock, if the lamb is too dry. ❧ Cover and cook for 30 minutes, or until the potatoes and meat are tender, stirring once or twice. ❧ Sprinkle with the cheese, stir briefly, and turn off the heat. ❧ Leave to stand for 4–5 minutes before serving.

Serves 4–5
Preparation: 15 minutes
Cooking: 1½ hours
Recipe grading: fairly easy

- 2 large scallions/spring onions or 1 small onion, thinly sliced
- 2½ tablespoons extra-virgin olive oil
- 2½ tablespoons rendered pork fat or finely chopped fresh pork fat
- 2 lb/1 kg lamb (from the shoulder or leg), cubed
- scant 1 cup/7 fl oz/200 ml dry red or dry white wine
- 1 tablespoon finely chopped parsley
- 2 cloves garlic, lightly crushed
- salt to taste
- freshly ground black pepper
- 1–1¼ cups/7–10 fl oz/200–300 ml hot stock (homemade or bouillon cube)
- 1¾ lb/800 g small new potatoes or large potatoes, diced
- ¾ cup/3 oz/90 g very coarsely grated pecorino (or caciocavallo) cheese

Suggested wine: a dry, full-bodied red (Etna rosso)

Lamb, cooked in many different ways, is a traditional Easter dish all over Italy. In Sicily, a little local cheese is often added to the cooking juices for extra flavor.

Farsumaru
Stuffed Beef Roll

Serves 6
Preparation: 30 minutes
Cooking: 1¼ hours
Recipe grading: fairly easy

- 4 oz/125 g ground lean beef or veal
- 7 oz/200 g Italian sausage meat
- 1 egg
- ½ cup/2 oz/60 g grated pecorino cheese
- 1 tablespoon finely chopped parsley
- 1½ tablespoons finely chopped onion
- 2 cloves garlic, finely chopped
- salt to taste
- freshly ground black pepper
- a single, thick slice of lean beef from top round, rib or chuck/topside, sirloin or chuck, weighing 1½ lb/750 g
- 7 oz/200 g prosciutto or ham, sliced
- 4 slices pancetta, chopped
- 3 hard-cooked/hard-boiled eggs
- 4 oz/125 g mature provolone cheese, cut into narrow strips
- 4 tablespoons extra-virgin olive oil
- scant ½ cup/3½ fl oz/100 ml dry red wine
- 1 tablespoon tomato paste, diluted in 1 cup/8 fl oz/250 ml hot water

Suggested wine: a dry red (Corvo rosso)

This long roll, with its rich, hidden filling, is equally delicious served hot straight from the pan or at room temperature.

Mix the ground beef and sausage meat in a large mixing bowl. ᔡ Add the raw egg, pecorino, parsley, onion, garlic, salt and pepper, and combine well. ᔡ Place the slice of beef flat between 2 sheets of parchment paper and beat gently until it is about ¼ in/5 mm thick. Be careful not to tear it. ᔡ Lay the meat out flat and cover with the prosciutto and pancetta. Spread the ground meat mixture over the top, leaving a narrow border around the edge. ᔡ Slice the pointed ends off the eggs and place them "nose to tail" down the middle. ᔡ Lay the provolone cheese on either side of the eggs. ᔡ Carefully roll up, bringing one "long" side over the eggs. Tie with string at regular intervals. ᔡ Heat the oil in a large, flameproof casserole, and brown the meat roll all over. ᔡ Pour the wine over the top and cook, uncovered, until it has evaporated. ᔡ Add the diluted tomato paste. ᔡ Cover and simmer over a very low heat for about 1 hour, turning several times. ᔡ Just before serving, remove the string and transfer to a heated serving platter. ᔡ Carve at table into slices about ¾ in/2 cm thick, spooning some of the cooking liquid over each serving.

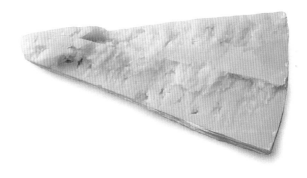

Serves 4
Preparation: 15 minutes
Cooking: 20–25 minutes
Recipe grading: easy

- 2 very fresh baby artichokes, trimmed and blanched, or 4–6 fresh or defrosted frozen artichoke hearts
- 4 slices of lean beef or veal from top round, rib or chuck steak/topside, sirloin or chuck steak, weighing about 1 lb/500 g in total
- salt to taste
- freshly ground black pepper
- ¼ cup/2 oz/60 g coarsely chopped prosciutto
- 3 tablespoons extra-virgin olive oil
- 1½ tablespoons finely chopped onion
- scant ½ cup/3½ fl oz/100 ml dry white wine

Suggested wine: a dry young white
(Bianco di Donnafugata)

Noultina

Stuffed Beef or Veal Rolls

See page 37 for preparation of the artichokes. ❧ Cut each baby artichoke from top to bottom into 6 slices (or quarter each artichoke heart). ❧ Place each slice of meat between 2 sheets of parchment paper and beat gently with a meat batter to flatten and enlarge it, taking care that it doesn't tear. Season with a little salt and plenty of pepper. ❧ Place 2 slices of fresh artichoke (or 1–1½ hearts) and a quarter of the prosciutto on each slice. Roll up and secure with toothpicks/cocktail sticks. ❧ Place in a heavy-bottomed saucepan with the oil and onion over a moderate heat and brown evenly all over, turning several times. ❧ Pour the wine over the rolls, cover tightly and cook over a low heat for 15–20 minutes. ❧ Serve very hot.

These rolls are very popular in Sicily and the recipe varies, not just from one village to another but from one household to the next. Each family has its own favorite stuffing and cooking method.

Purpetti

Meatballs in Tomato Sauce

Sauté the onion in the oil in a large, heavy-bottomed saucepan. Add the tomatoes, oregano, and salt. ✒ Cook, uncovered, over a moderate heat for 10 minutes. ✒ Place the breadcrumbs in a large mixing bowl with the milk. Stir in the meat and all the other ingredients, season with salt and pepper, and mix very thoroughly. ✒ Shape into meatballs and add to the hot tomato sauce. Simmer for 15–20 minutes, turning carefully once or twice. ✒ Serve very hot.

Serves 4
Preparation: 15 minutes
Cooking: 25–30 minutes
Recipe grading: easy

To make the sauce:

- 2 tablespoons finely chopped onion
- 3 tablespoons extra-virgin olive oil
- 14 oz/400 g fresh or canned Italian tomatoes, skinned and chopped
- 1 teaspoon oregano (or 6 fresh basil leaves)
- salt to taste

For the meatballs:

- 1 cup/2 oz/60 g breadcrumbs
- 4 tablespoons milk
- 3½ cups/14 oz/400 g ground beef or veal
- scant 1 cup/3½ oz/100 g freshly grated pecorino or mature caciocavallo cheese
- 2 eggs
- 1 tablespoon finely chopped onion
- 1 tablespoon finely chopped parsley
- 1 clove garlic, finely chopped
- salt to taste
- freshly ground black pepper

Suggested wine: a young rosé (Etna rosato)

For a different, but equally delicious dish, thread the meatballs onto skewers, alternating them with cubes of 2-day-old bread and half bay leaves and broil (grill), basting at frequent intervals with olive oil. When cooked, spoon the tomato sauce over the top and serve.

Cunigghiu all'Auruduci

Rabbit in Sweet and Sour Sauce

Put the wine, parsley, onion, bay leaf, and peppercorns in a small saucepan and bring slowly to a boil. Boil for 1 minute, take off the heat, and set aside to cool. ❧ Place the pieces of rabbit in a large mixing bowl. Pour the wine marinade over them and leave to marinate for 6–8 hours. ❧ Remove the rabbit from the marinade and dry with paper towels. Season lightly with salt and pepper and coat with flour, shaking off the excess. ❧ Heat the oil in a wide nonstick skillet until it is very hot. Add the pieces of rabbit and brown well all over. ❧ Sprinkle lightly with salt and pepper each time you turn them. This stage will take about 10 minutes. ❧ Remove the browned rabbit from the pan and set aside. ❧ In the same oil, sauté the onion, celery, carrot, capers, raisins, and olives for 5 minutes over a moderate heat, stirring frequently. ❧ Add the rabbit and sprinkle with sugar. Pour in the vinegar. (If using honey, mix it with the vinegar first.) ❧ After 2 minutes, add about 1 cup/8 fl oz/250 ml of the strained marinade, cover and simmer over a low heat, turning the rabbit and adding more marinade at intervals, until it is very tender. ❧ Serve hot.

This is a classic dish in the Sicilian repertoire. The original recipe calls for wild rabbit but nowadays these can be difficult to buy, and farmed rabbit is used instead. If preferred, replace the rabbit with a tender young chicken.

Serves 4–6

Preparation: 30 minutes + 6–8 hours' marinating

Cooking: 1¼ hours

Recipe grading: fairly easy

- 1¼ cups/10 fl oz/300 ml dry red wine
- 3–4 sprigs parsley
- 1 medium onion, sliced
- 1 bay leaf
- 1 teaspoon black peppercorns
- 1 young, tender rabbit, cleaned and cut into 6–8 pieces (minus the head – ask your butcher to do it)
- salt to taste
- freshly ground black pepper
- 3 tablespoons all-purpose/plain flour
- 6 tablespoons extra-virgin olive oil
- 1 medium onion, thinly sliced
- 2 stalks celery, coarsely chopped
- 1 small carrot, sliced
- 1 tablespoon capers
- 2½ tablespoons seedless white raisins/sultanas, briefly soaked
- 15 large green olives, pitted and coarsely chopped
- 2 tablespoons sugar (or Acacia honey)
- 4 tablespoons Italian red wine vinegar

Suggested wine: a dry rosé (Rosé di Fontanarossa)

Capretto al Limone

Braised Kid with Lemon

Serves 4–5
Preparation: 10 minutes
Cooking: 1 hour
Recipe grading: fairly easy

- generous ¼ cup/2½ oz/75 g rendered pork fat or finely chopped fresh pork fat
- 2 lb/1 kg kid meat, cut into small pieces
- salt to taste
- freshly ground black pepper
- 1¾ cups/14 fl oz/400 ml hot stock (homemade or bouillon cube)
- juice of 2 lemons

Suggested wine: a dry white (Corvo)

Melt the pork fat over a low heat in a flameproof earthenware casserole. Add the meat and season with salt and pepper. ↝ Moisten with some of the hot stock. Cover and cook in a preheated oven at 350°F/180°C/gas 4 for about 1 hour or until the meat is very tender, basting at frequent intervals with a little more hot stock. ↝ Drizzle with the lemon juice and serve hot.

This dish is equally good when made with tender young lamb.

A word about the wine: there are two schools of thought on serving wine with dishes with a strong lemon flavor. The first, rather severe one, outlaws it totally; the second, more tolerant school, is of the opinion that many lemon dishes are enhanced when accompanied by the right wine.

Agnello alle Olive
Braised Lamb with Olives

Serves 4–5
Preparation: 10 minutes
Cooking: 1 hour
Recipe grading: fairly easy

Place the lamb in a flameproof earthenware casserole. Drizzle with the oil and season with salt and a generous sprinkling of pepper. Sprinkle with the olives and moisten with half the wine. ☙ Cover and cook in a preheated oven at 350°F/180°C/gas 4 for about 1 hour or until the meat is very tender, basting at frequent intervals with a little more wine.

- 2 lb/1 kg lamb, cut into fairly small pieces
- 3½ tablespoons extra-virgin olive oil
- salt to taste
- freshly ground black pepper
- 1½ cups /7 oz/200 g large black olives, pitted and cut into quarters
- 1¼ cups/10 fl oz/300 ml dry red wine

Suggested wine: a dry, full-bodied red (Etna rosso)

In Sicily this dish is often made with kid, or baby goat's meat (sometimes marketed in the U.S. as chevron). Both the delicate flavor of kid and the stronger taste of lamb work well with the olives.

Sicilian Wines

The hot, dry climate of Sicily ensures that its wines are full bodied and aromatic with a very definite character. The island's viticulture dates back to around the 14th century BC. At that time wine growers in the Agrigento area carried on a flourishing export trade with merchants in Mycenaean Greece. A wine jug dating from that era was found in the necropolis of Cozzo Pantano (now Syracuse). Another vessel bearing the inscription VIINO and dating from the 5th century BC, has come to light in the province of Enna.

The most famous and typical of all Sicilian wines, Marsala was the brainchild of an Englishman. During the second half of the 18th century, John Woodhouse visited Sicily and, having tasted the local wine, decided to use it as the basis for an alternative to the immensely popular and

fashionable Madeira wine. His original formula was subsequently modified by Benjamin Ingham in the early 19th century, with the addition of cooked, concentrated musts.

Marsala is produced in the area around the port town of the same name in the province of Trapani. It is made with very carefully selected grapes, mainly the Cataratto and Inzolia varieties, which have a high sugar content. Marsala has a strength of 15-16 degrees when young, rising as high as 20 degrees and acquiring its characteristic flavor when aged. It has a very pronounced taste and a distinctive aroma. It is classified as "virgin" before the addition of the concia (consisting of a must made with partially dried grapes mixed with raw spirit to halt fermentation [known as the sifone] and cotto, a must which has been cooked and reduced to only one-third of its original volume). This process endows the wine with its instantly recognizable character and allows it to age successfully.

Marsala labels carry the following descriptions depending on how long they have been aged in the cask: Fine (one year), Superiore (*two years*), Superiore Riserva (*four years*), Vergine (*five years*), and Virgine Riserva (*ten years*). There is a choice of Secco (*dry*); Semisecco (*medium*), or Dolce (*sweet*), depending on the sugar content of the wine. Color varies and is described as Oro (*gold*) if natural; Ambra (*amber*) after the addition of a small quantity of cotto (*a very dark caramel which looks like black treacle, made by boiling and reducing grape juice*), and Ruby when red.

Two other DOC wines besides Marsala are produced in the Trapani region: one is Bianco Alcamo, *a pale, straw-yellow wine which with its dry, fruity, full flavor goes very well with fish. The other is* Moscato di Pantelleria, *a sweet, amber-colored wine made from the superb Muscatel grape, an ideal wine to serve with the dessert course or on its own.* Donnafugata, *a light, everyday wine which can be white, rosé or red, is also produced in this area.*

Only one DOC wine is made in the province of Ragusa, but it is an exceptional one: Cerasuolo *is a beautiful cherry red color and has a warm, dry, harmonious taste. It is best drunk with meat, especially broiled (grilled) meats and game. Another DOC* Cerasuolo *wine is produced in the province of Caltanissetta; this one is called* Cerasuolo di Vittoria.

Moscato (*Siracusa and Noto*) *wine is also produced near Syracuse, while in the province of Catania, a DOC wine called* Etna *is made, which can be red, rosé or white. These wines are all around 12 degrees in strength and have full, pronounced, and harmonious aromas and tastes. They age well, the red up to seven years and the white up to three years.*

In the province of Messina a noteworthy DOC wine called Malvasia di Lipari *is produced. Sweet and aromatic, it is best drunk when it has aged for at least eight years.*

Another Etna wine which merits its DOC appellation is made in the Agrigento area where some very fine grapes flourish. The Etna white wines, Bianco *and* Bianco Superiore *and the* Rosato (*rosé*) *are best drunk at around three years old, while the red ages well up to seven years.*

The area around Palermo is home to some of the most respected wine companies (Duca di Salaparuta, Tasca di Almerita), and many fine wines are made there.

In Italy many good wines are labelled DOC or DOCG, meaning Denominazione di origine controllata *and* Denominazione di origine controllata e garantita, *respectively. This means that they were produced in clearly defined geographical zones on approved vineyards.*

Agnello con Patate

Lamb and Potato Casserole

Serves 4

Preparation: 15 minutes

Cooking: 1 hour

Recipe grading: fairly easy

- 2 lb/1 kg lamb, cut into fairly small pieces
- 1½ lb/750 g yellow, waxy potatoes, thickly sliced or in wedges
- 3 large fresh tomatoes, quartered or cut into 6 pieces
- 1 medium onion, sliced
- 4 tablespoons extra-virgin olive oil
- salt to taste
- freshly ground black pepper
- leaves from a small sprig of fresh rosemary
- 1 teaspoon oregano

Suggested wine: a dry, full-bodied red (Etna rosso)

Place the meat, potatoes, tomatoes, and onion in an ovenproof earthenware casserole. ❧ Drizzle with the oil and season with a little salt and plenty of pepper. Sprinkle with the rosemary and oregano. ❧ Cover and cook in a preheated oven at 400°F/200°C/gas 6 for about 1 hour or until very tender, basting at frequent intervals with a little hot water. ❧ Serve hot.

Anciova a Catanisa

Anchovies Catania-Style

Serves 4–5
Preparation: 30 minutes
Cooking: 30 minutes
Recipe grading: fairly easy

- 1½ lb/750 g fresh anchovies
- 4 tablespoons extra-virgin olive oil
- salt to taste
- freshly ground black pepper
- 1 lemon, thinly sliced (organic, not treated with fungicide)
- 12 green olives, pitted and coarsely chopped
- 2½ tablespoons pine nuts
- scant ½ cup/3½ fl oz/100 ml dry white wine
- ⅓ cup/1 oz/30 g fine dry breadcrumbs
- juice of 1 orange

Suggested wine: a light, dry white (Bianco Alcamo)

Clean the anchovies, gently pulling off their heads (the viscera will come away with the head), and slit them down their bellies so that they can be opened out flat. Remove their backbones, rinse and pat dry with paper towels. ❧ Use half the oil to grease a round, shallow ovenproof dish in which the anchovies will fit snugly when arranged in two layers. ❧ Place half the anchovies in the dish, tails toward the center, fanned out like the spokes of a wheel, overlapping if necessary. ❧ Season with a little salt and pepper, then place the lemon slices on top. Scatter with half the olives and pine nuts and drizzle with half the remaining oil. ❧ Cover with a second layer of anchovies and the remaining olives and pine nuts. Drizzle with the wine and sprinkle with the breadcrumbs. ❧ Drizzle with the remaining oil and cook in a preheated oven at 350°F/180°C/gas 4 for 15 minutes. ❧ Remove the dish from the oven, drizzle with the orange juice, and return to the oven for 15 minutes. ❧ Serve hot or warm.

The humble anchovy is transformed into a real treat when prepared in this way .

Calamari Affucati
Braised Squid

Sauté the onion and garlic in the oil in a heavy-bottomed saucepan. ❧ Add the squid and cook for 2–3 minutes, then pour in the wine. Cover and simmer gently over a low heat for 15–20 minutes. Stir ocassionally and check that the squid doesn't dry out; they usually release enough liquid, but it may be necessary to add a little water as they cook. ❧ Stir in the tomatoes, olives, capers, parsley, celery, chili pepper, and salt. ❧ Cover and simmer gently for 40 minutes, or until the squid is very tender. ❧ Serve hot or at room temperature.

Serves 4
Preparation: 20 minutes
Cooking: about 1 hour
Recipe grading: easy

- 1½ tablespoons finely chopped onion
- 1 clove garlic, lightly crushed
- 4 tablespoons extra-virgin olive oil
- 1¼ lb/625 g squid (cleaned and prepared weight – ask your fish vendor to prepare it), coarsely chopped
- scant ½ cup/3½ fl oz/100 ml dry white wine
- 3 fresh or canned tomatoes, skinned and coarsely chopped
- 10 green olives, pitted and coarsely chopped
- 1 tablespoon capers
- 1 tablespoon finely chopped parsley
- 2 tender stalks celery, trimmed and very thinly sliced
- ½ dried chili pepper, seeded and crumbled
- salt to taste

Suggested wine: a dry white (Alcamo)

The delicate flavor of the squid and olives is enhanced by the firey chili pepper. Start by adding a little then taste during cooking to see whether you want to use more.

Serves 4
Preparation: 30 minutes
Cooking: 20–25 minutes
Recipe grading: fairly easy

- 1¹/₂–1³/₄ lb/700–800 g very fresh (or defrosted frozen) large sardines
- ¹/₂ cup/4 fl oz/125 ml extra-virgin olive oil
- 1³/₄ cups/3¹/₂ oz/100 g fresh breadcrumbs
- 5 salted anchovies (rinsed and boned) or 8–10 anchovy fillets
- 2¹/₂ tablespoons seedless white raisins/sultanas, soaked and drained
- 2¹/₂ tablespoons pine nuts
- 1 tablespoon capers
- 5 large black olives, pitted and chopped
- 1 tablespoon finely chopped parsley
- 1 tablespoon lemon juice
- finely grated zest/rind of ¹/₂ lemon
- 1 teaspoon sugar
- salt to taste
- freshly ground black pepper
- bay leaves

Suggested wine: a dry white
(Bianco di Donnafugata)

Sardi a Beccaficu
Palermo-Style Stuffed Sardine Rolls

Scale the sardines and remove the heads and viscera. Use kitchen scissors to slit them along their bellies, remove the bones, and open them out flat. Rinse and dry with paper towels. ❧ Heat 4 tablespoons of the oil in a wide, nonstick skillet over a moderate heat and add two-thirds of the breadcrumbs. Stir for 1–2 minutes, then set aside in a mixing bowl. ❧ Pour 1 tablespoon of fresh oil into the skillet and add the anchovies, crushing them with a fork over a low heat so that they turn into a paste. ❧ Stir into the breadcrumbs, followed by the raisins, pine nuts, capers, olives, parsley, lemon juice and zest, sugar, a little salt and a generous sprinkling of pepper. Mix well. ❧ Lay the sardines out flat, skin side downward, and spread some of the mixture on each. ❧ Roll the sardines up, starting at the head end, and place in an oiled ovenproof dish. Pack them closely together, tail downward, and wedge a bay leaf between each one. ❧ Sprinkle with the remaining breadcrumbs and drizzle with the remaining oil. ❧ Bake in a preheated oven at 400°F/200°C/ gas 6 for 20–25 minutes. ❧ Serve hot or at room temperature.

For Catanese-Style Sardines, replace half the breadcrumbs with grated pecorino cheese and a little chopped onion or garlic. Spread a little of this mixture on each sardine. Lay another sardine on top, skin-side-up and firmly press together. Dip in beaten egg, coat with breadcrumbs, and fry in olive oil until golden brown and crisp. Serve hot.

Murruzzi a Palermitana

Hake Palermo-Style

Serves 4
Preparation: 20 minutes
Cooking: 25 minutes
Recipe grading: easy

- 4 salted anchovies (rinsed and boned) or 6–8 anchovy fillets
- 4 tablespoons extra-virgin olive oil
- 2 whole, small hake, each weighing about 1½ lb/750 g, gutted
- 3–4 tablespoons breadcrumbs
- 1 tablespoon finely chopped parsley
- 1 teaspoon very finely chopped fresh rosemary leaves
- freshly ground black pepper
- lemon slices or wedges

Suggested wine: a dry white (Etna bianco)

Place the anchovies in a small skillet with 1½ tablespoons of the oil over a low heat. Stir and crush them with a fork until they dissolve in the oil. ❧ Spread half this mixture inside the cavities of the hake and the remainder over their outside surfaces. ❧ Mix the breadcrumbs, parsley, rosemary, and a generous sprinkling of pepper on a large plate and coat the fish all over. ❧ Grease an ovenproof dish or roasting pan with 1½ tablespoons of the oil and place the fish in it. Drizzle with the remaining oil and bake in a preheated oven at 375°F/190°C/gas 5 for 25 minutes. ❧ Serve very hot, garnished with lemon.

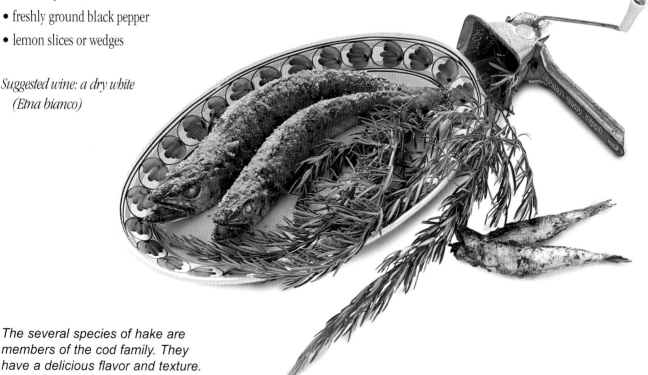

The several species of hake are members of the cod family. They have a delicious flavor and texture.

Palummu a Scapeci

Fried Shark Steaks with Savory Topping

Serves 4
Preparation: 10 minutes
Cooking: 30 minutes
Recipe grading: easy

Season both sides of the shark steaks with a little salt and pepper and coat them lightly with flour. ❧ Heat the oil in a large, nonstick skillet until it is very hot. Add the steaks and fry over a moderately high heat, browning them well on both sides. ❧ Remove from the skillet and in the same oil sauté the onion and the garlic until soft. Add the tomato and cook for 10 minutes over a low heat, then add the pine nuts, raisins, and parsley. ❧ Stir well and then return the steaks to the pan. Cover and simmer over a low heat for 10–15 minutes, turning once. ❧ Remove from the heat and set aside to cool for at least 2–3 hours so that the fish can absorb all the flavors. ❧ Serve at room temperature.

- 4 shark steaks, about $^3/_4$ in/2 cm thick
- salt to taste
- freshly ground black pepper
- 2$^1/_2$ tablespoons all-purpose/plain flour
- 6 tablespoons extra-virgin olive oil
- 1 medium onion, very thinly sliced
- 1–2 cloves garlic, crushed or coarsely chopped
- 1 large fresh tomato, skinned and chopped
- 1$^1/_2$ tablespoons pine nuts
- 1$^1/_2$ tablespoons seedless white raisins/sultanas, soaked and drained
- 1 tablespoon coarsely chopped parsley

Suggested wine: a young dry white
(Bianco di Donnafugata)

In Sicily very small sharks are sold whole. These are usually smooth dogfish (smooth hound) and the flesh is very tender, with a delicate taste. There are many versions of this recipe in Italian cooking, varying from region to region.

Tunnu Riganatu

Fresh Tuna with Oregano

Place the tomatoes in a mixing bowl with the garlic, capers, oregano, a little salt, and a generous sprinkling of pepper. ❧ Rinse the tuna and dry with paper towels. ❧ Pour just over half the oil into a wide ovenproof dish and arrange the tuna slices in a single layer. ❧ Cover with the tomato mixture and drizzle with the remaining oil. Cook in a preheated oven at 350°F/ 180°C/gas 4 for about 30 minutes.

Serves 4
Preparation: 10 minutes
Cooking: 30 minutes
Recipe grading: easy

- 14 oz/400 g fresh or canned tomatoes, skinned and chopped
- 1 clove garlic, finely chopped
- 1 tablespoon capers
- 1 teaspoon oregano
- salt to taste
- freshly ground black pepper
- 4 slices of very fresh tuna, each weighing about 5–6 oz/150–180 g, preferably taken from the belly of the fish
- scant ¹/₂ cup/3¹/₂ fl oz/100 ml extra-virgin olive oil

Suggested wine: a dry white (Alcamo)

This recipe comes from Italian food writer Giuseppe Coria's excellent book: Profumi di Sicilia *('A Taste of Sicily') and is a perfect example of the quintessential aromas and flavors of Sicilian cooking.*

The Influence of the Arab World

The Arabs, or Saracens as they are also known, dominated Sicily for around two hundred and fifty years, from 827 onward. Astute traders and able administrators, they changed the face of Sicily and under their rule the island experienced a period of prosperity. Commerce flourished, the island's ports were expanded and there was an extraordinary flowering of cultural life. Arable farming was developed and diversified, due largely to the Arabs' skill in the construction of irrigation systems. A fishing technique used for catching tuna, first introduced by the Phoenicians, was greatly improved. Sicily flourished under the Arabs and many reminders of their presence have survived intact to the present day.

Puppets of the characters from the Old French epic poem The Chanson de Roland *have become a part of the Sicilian tradition. The poem tells of the battle the medieval king Charlemagne fought against the Arabs in Spain in 778.*

The cloister of the Benedictine monastery at Monreale, near Palermo, shows strong Arab influence. Although the strikingly beautiful cathedral and monastery were built in 1174, after the Saracens had surrendered power to the Normans, Arab taste mingles in the architecture with Norman, Byzantine, and Italian styles.

The red domes of the church of San Giovanni degli Eremiti in Palermo date from Arab-Norman times.

The Arabs introduced a number of new foods, including oriental spices such as cinnamon and saffron, and citrus fruits. Rice was another new arrival and, although not widely cultivated as the terrain was unsuitable, it became an important ingredient in Sicilian cooking. Arancini or *Stuffed Rice Ball Fritters* (see recipe, page 18) entered the culinary repertoire at this time. The Saracens also brought sugar cane to the island, as well as cotton, prickly pears, and jasmine, and they taught the Sicilians how to dry figs and grapes. Dried pasta also dates back to this period, but it is open to question whether the Arabs or Sicilians can claim credit for its invention.

The mixed sweet and sour flavor so evident in many Sicilian dishes is also part of the Arabian culinary legacy, as was couscous which remains a typical dish of the port of Trapani in western Sicily.

Skilled pastrycooks, the Arabs introduced marzipan and cakes made with honey, and inspired the invention of the famous Cassata (the name comes from the Arabic quas'at, meaning a deep bowl). Cassata later underwent several transformations, one being the addition of chocolate after the European discovery of South America. By the late 1550s, long before the rest of Europe learnt how to process cocoa into solid blocks, Sicilian confectioners had already perfected the technique in Modica (Ragusa), although the end product differed from the chocolate produced elsewhere. It retains its special texture and taste to this day.

The Arabs are credited with the invention of sorbets or water ices, the forerunners of today's ices; these were made with snow from the slopes of Etna, flavored and scented with fruit and flowers, but it is thought likely that the ancient Romans were already making similar refreshments centuries earlier.

Tunnu Arrustutu

Broiled Fresh Tuna Steaks

Serves 4

Preparation: 5 minutes + 30–40 minutes' marinating

Cooking: 8–10 minutes

Recipe grading: easy

- 4 tuna steaks, weighing about 7 oz/ 200 g each
- ²/₃ cup/5 fl oz/150 ml extra-virgin olive oil
- 1¼ tablespoons oregano
- salt to taste
- freshly ground black pepper

Suggested wine: a young dry Marsala (Marsala Vergine)

Rinse the tuna steaks and dry on paper towels. ❧ Mix the oil, oregano, salt, and pepper, and pour over the steaks. Set aside to marinate for 30–40 minutes. ❧ Take the steaks out of the marinade just before they are to be cooked. ❧ Heat the broiler/grill or barbecue to very hot and cook the steaks for 4–5 minutes each side. While they are cooking, especially if you are barbecuing them, keep moist with plenty of the marinade. ❧ When cooked, spoon a little more marinade over the top and serve very hot.

Fresh tuna steaks are particularly good when barbecued or broiled/grilled. In Italy a special type of hinged broiler/toaster is used, the two halves holding the steak securely in place. A heavy, nonstick, ridged broiling/grilling pan or a traditional broiler/grill can also be used.

Pisci Spata che Sarmorigghiu

Broiled Swordfish with Lemon Sauce

Serves 4
Preparation: 10 minutes
Cooking: 8–10 minutes
Recipe grading: easy

Pour about half the oil into a small blender and gradually add the hot water and lemon juice, processing continuously as you do so. ᴓ Put into a small heatproof bowl. (Alternatively, place the oil in a small, heatproof bowl and gradually beat in the water and juice with a balloon whisk, adding a little at a time.) ᴓ Stir in the parsley, garlic, oregano, salt, and pepper. ᴓ Place the bowl over a pan of boiling water to heat for 3–4 minutes before serving. ᴓ Coat the swordfish steaks with the remaining oil and broil/grill or barbecue them for 4–5 minutes on each side. ᴓ Serve immediately, handing round the sauce separately in a heated jug.

- ²⁄₃ cup/5 fl oz/150 ml extra-virgin olive oil
- 4 tablespoons hot water
- 6 tablespoons fresh lemon juice
- 1 tablespoon finely chopped parsley
- 1 clove garlic, finely chopped
- 2 teaspoons oregano
- salt to taste
- freshly ground black pepper
- 4 steaks or slices of swordfish weighing about 5–6 oz/150–180 g each, preferably from the belly of the fish

Suggested wine: a light dry white
(Alcamo Rincione)

Superb fresh swordfish is sold in markets all over Sicily. It can be prepared in a variety of ways; this is a very traditional recipe. The lemon sauce is typically Sicilian and can also be served with other broiled/grilled fish and meat dishes.

Baccalà a Sfinciuni

Baked Salt Cod

Serves 4
Preparation: 15 minutes
Cooking: 45 minutes
Recipe grading: easy

Use about half the oil to grease a wide, shallow ovenproof dish. ॐ Arrange the pieces of cod in a single layer and cover with the potatoes. ॐ Sprinkle with the parsley, onion, garlic, oregano, very little salt, and a generous sprinkling of pepper. Sprinkle with the breadcrumbs and drizzle with the remaining oil. ॐ Bake in a preheated oven at 350°F/180°C/gas 4 for about 45 minutes, or until the potatoes and fish are tender.

- 4 tablespoons extra-virgin olive oil
- 1½ lb/750 g pre-soaked salt cod, cut into pieces
- 1½ lb/750 g potatoes, cut into fairly large cubes
- 1 tablespoon finely chopped parsley
- 1 medium onion, thinly sliced
- 2 cloves garlic, finely chopped
- 1 teaspoon oregano
- salt to taste
- freshly ground black pepper
- 4 tablespoons fine dry breadcrumbs

Suggested wine: a young rosé (Etna rosato)

Be sure to buy salt cod that is pre-soaked and ready to cook. To prepare it for cooking, remove the bones, rinse briefly, and pat dry with paper towels or a clean dish cloth. Cut the cod crosswise into slices about 2 in/5 cm wide. Leave the skin on, as this helps to prevent it flaking and breaking up during cooking.

Piscistuocco a Ghiotta

Stockfish Messina-Style

Serves 4
Preparation: 10 minutes
Cooking: 1¹/₂ hours
Recipe grading: fairly easy

- 1¹/₂ lb/750 g pre-soaked stockfish, with bones and fins removed
- ¹/₂ cup/4 fl oz/125 ml extra-virgin olive oil
- 1 medium onion, finely chopped
- 1 whole clove garlic, lightly crushed
- 2¹/₂ tablespoons all-purpose/plain flour
- salt to taste
- freshly ground black pepper
- 14 oz/400 g fresh or canned tomatoes, skinned and chopped
- 1¹/₄ lb/625 g potatoes, peeled and sliced about ¹/₄ in/5 mm thick
- 2 slightly underripe pears, peeled, cored and sliced (optional)
- 1¹/₄ cups/5 oz/150 g green olives, pitted
- 2 small, tender celery stalks, sliced
- 1–2 tablespoons capers
- 2¹/₂ tablespoons pine nuts
- 2¹/₂ tablespoons seedless white raisins/sultanas, soaked and drained

Suggested wine: a dry white (Alcamo)

Rinse the stockfish and dry with paper towels. Cut into pieces roughly 3 in/ 8 cm square. ❧ Pour the oil into a flameproof casserole dish and sauté the onion and garlic. Do not let them color. ❧ Coat the pieces of stockfish lightly with flour and cook for a few minutes over a slightly higher heat, turning them once. ❧ Season with a little salt and pepper. ❧ Add the tomatoes and sufficient hot water to just cover the fish. ❧ Cover and simmer over a moderate heat for 45 minutes. ❧ Add the potatoes, pears, if using, olives, celery, capers, pine nuts, and raisins. ❧ Stir carefully, cover and cook for another 40 minutes. ❧ There should be plenty of liquid left when the fish is cooked. If not, moisten with hot water as necessary.

*Like salt cod, stockfish should also be bought pre-soaked.
To prepare, remove the bones and fins. You may leave
the skin on during cooking or remove, as preferred.*

Verdure

Sicilian vegetables are always exceptionally good, with subtle flavors that greens grown elsewhere seem to lack. They are cultivated all over the island and no meal is complete without its vegetable side dish or garnish. With the exception of tomatoes, which find their way into a great many sauces and other recipes, eggplants are perhaps the most widely used vegetable, undergoing a dizzying number of transformations. Globe artichokes are also extremely popular, as are bell peppers (sweet peppers or capsicums). Mushrooms are more typical of the mountainous, inland areas of the island.

Funci 'Ncartati

Mushrooms Cooked in Foil Packages

Place the cheese, breadcrumbs, anchovies, garlic, parsley, lemon juice, salt, pepper, and half of the oil in a mixing bowl and mix thoroughly. ❧ Place each mushroom cap upside down on a fairly large piece of oiled foil. ❧ Spread an equal part of the mixture over each mushroom. ❧ Bring two sides of the foil up over each mushroom to make a pleat, leaving plenty of air space inside, and fold the ends over. ❧ When you have packaged all the mushrooms, place on a baking sheet in a preheated oven at 375°F/190°C/ gas 5 and cook for 20–25 minutes, depending on the size of the mushrooms. ❧ If using smaller porcini place two in each package. The small porcini and the other types of mushrooms will take only about 15–20 minutes to cook.

Serves 4
Preparation: 15 minutes
Cooking: 20–25 minutes
Recipe grading: easy

- 5 tablespoons freshly grated pecorino cheese
- 3 tablespoons breadcrumbs
- 2 salted anchovies (rinsed and boned) or 4 anchovy fillets, finely chopped
- 2 cloves garlic, finely chopped
- 2½ tablespoons finely chopped parsley
- 1 teaspoon lemon juice
- salt to taste
- freshly ground black pepper
- scant ½ cup/3½ fl oz/100 ml extra-virgin olive oil
- 4 large or 8 small porcini mushroom caps (or large horse, field, or cultivated mushrooms), cleaned

Suggested wine: a dry red (Sciacca)

This recipe comes from the Agrigento area where mushrooms, wrapped in moistened butchers' wrapping paper, used to be buried in the hot ashes in the fireplace or placed on a grill above the glowing embers.

Capunata di Caciuocculi

Sweet-Sour Artichokes

Serves 4
Preparation: 15 minutes
Cooking: 35–40 minutes
Recipe grading: easy

- 8 very young, fresh artichokes
- 2½ tablespoons all-purpose/plain flour
- 6 tablespoons extra-virgin olive oil
- 2½ tablespoons finely chopped onion
- 1 tablespoon capers
- 12 green olives, pitted and chopped
- 1 small carrot, diced
- 2 tender stalks celery, trimmed and thinly sliced
- salt to taste
- freshly ground black pepper
- scant ½ cup/3½ fl oz/100 ml hot water
- 4 medium tomatoes
- 2 salted anchovies (rinsed and boned) or 4 anchovy fillets
- 4 tablespoons Italian wine vinegar
- 2½ teaspoons sugar

Suggested wine: a young, dry white (Bianco di Donnafugata)

Prepare the artichokes as described on page 37. Cut each artichoke lengthwise into six sections. ✑ Coat the artichokes lightly with flour and fry in a flameproof casserole over a fairly high heat for 2–3 minutes, turning once or twice. ✑ Remove the artichokes, letting the excess oil drain back into the casserole. ✑ Add the onion, capers, olives, carrot, celery, salt, pepper, and hot water and simmer over a moderate heat for about 10 minutes. ✑ Stir in the tomatoes and then add the artichokes and anchovies. Cover and simmer over a low heat for 20–25 minutes. ✑ Mix the sugar with the vinegar and stir into the vegetables. Leave to cook for a final 4–5 minutes. ✑ Serve warm or at room temperature.

This is a variation on the classic Sicilian Capunata (see recipe, page 24).

Flavors and Aromas

S icily's warm Mediterranean climate is ideal for the wide range of herbs and other aromas and flavorings that are an essential part of its cuisine. Aromatic herbs (many of which grow wild), such as basil, oregano, bay leaves, mint, chives, marjoram, sage, rosemary, parsley, wild fennel, and many others, flourish and acquire especially intense, unique fragrances. Olives, and almonds and other nuts, are plentiful and are consumed whole or chopped (to flavor dishes), or are pressed into delicious oils. Citrus fruit grows well all over the island and the flesh or zest (rind) is used fresh or candied in a wide range of dishes. Various honeys add extra, subtle dimensions (depending on the flowers from which the bees have harvested the nectar) to cakes and desserts.

Wild thyme honey is one of the best of the countless varieties. In ancient Roman times it was considered auspicious for newlyweds to be given gifts of honey during the four weeks following their wedding and this gave rise to the word "honeymoon," the first, joyous and carefree days of marriage. In some parts of Sicily newlyweds still receive gifts of honey.

Capers

Juniper berries

Pistacchios

Pine nuts

Almonds

Orange

Green and black olives

Lemons

94

Oregano

Thyme

Chilies

Garlic

Chives

Marjoram

Flat-leaf parsley

Rosemary

Sage

Wild fennel

Mint

Bay leaves

Basil

Milinciani a Beccaficu

Fried Eggplant and Cheese "Sandwiches"

Serves 4

Preparation: 20 minutes + 1 hour for degorging the eggplants

Cooking: 10 minutes

Recipe grading: easy

- 4 medium eggplants/aubergines, preferably long thin ones
- coarse sea salt
- 2 eggs
- salt to taste
- freshly ground black pepper
- 3–4 salted anchovies (rinsed and boned) or 6–8 anchovy fillets, coarsely chopped
- 4 oz/125 g semi-hard pecorino cheese, cut into short thin strips
- 15–20 fresh basil leaves, torn
- scant ¾ cup/2 oz/60 g breadcrumbs
- extra-virgin olive oil (or ordinary good quality olive oil) for frying

Suggested wine: a dry red (Rosso di Donnafugata)

Cut the eggplants across their width into slices about ¼ in/ 5 mm thick. Place in a colander, sprinkle with salt, and leave to stand for at least 1 hour. ⇒ Rinse and dry with paper towels. ⇒ Beat the eggs lightly with a little salt and pepper in a fairly wide, shallow bowl. ⇒ Make the "sandwiches" by selecting two slices of eggplant of similar size and filling each pair with a few pieces of cheese, 2–3 anchovy pieces, and some basil. ⇒ Press the slices firmly together, carefully dip them into the egg, and then coat with breadcrumbs. Make sure that the edges are stuck together. ⇒ Heat at least ¾ in/2 cm of oil in a large nonstick skillet until it is very hot. Fry 2–3 sandwiches at a time until they are golden brown on both sides. ⇒ Serve hot.

Eggplants are plentiful throughout the long Sicilian summers and are prepared in all sorts of ways. This recipe originated in the Enna region.

Pipi 'Nfurnati
Baked Bell Peppers

Slice the bell peppers from top to bottom into quarters. Remove the stalks and surrounding hard parts, and the white pith and seeds. ☙ Rinse the bell peppers quickly and dry well. Slice into strips ½ in/1 cm wide and put into a large mixing bowl. ☙ Add the olives, anchovies, pine nuts, capers, and basil. ☙ Add 5 tablespoons of the oil and a little salt and mix thoroughly, as if you were tossing a salad. ☙ Grease a wide, fairly deep ovenproof dish with the remaining oil and put the bell pepper mixture into it, pressing down gently. It should form a layer about 1½ in/4 cm deep. ☙ Sprinkle with the breadcrumbs and bake in a preheated oven at 350°F/180°C/gas 4 for 30–35 minutes, or until the strips of bell pepper are tender.

Serves 4
Preparation: 15 minutes
Cooking: 30–35 minutes
Recipe grading: easy

- 1 medium green bell pepper/capsicum
- 1 medium red bell pepper/capsicum
- 1 medium yellow bell pepper/capsicum
- 20 black olives, pitted and quartered
- 2–3 salted anchovies (rinsed and boned) or 4–6 anchovy fillets, coarsely chopped
- 4 tablespoons pine nuts
- 2 tablespoons capers
- 10–12 fresh basil leaves, torn
- 6 tablespoons extra-virgin olive oil
- salt to taste
- 4 tablespoons breadcrumbs

Suggested wine: a dry red
(Rosso di Donnafugata)

This brightly colored dish is delicious served hot but even better when it has been left to stand at room temperature for 2–3 hours after baking.

Carduni Fritti

Crumbed Fried Cardoons

Serves 4
Preparation: 10 minutes
Cooking: 30–40 minutes
Recipe grading: easy

Discard the tough outer stalks of the cardoons. Remove the strings from the inner stalks, rubbing the exposed surfaces with lemon to prevent them turning black. ❧ Cut the stalks into pieces about 4 in/10 cm long and boil in plenty of salted water for 20–30 minutes, or until tender. Test by piercing with a fork. ❧ Drain well. Coat with flour, dip in the egg seasoned with salt and pepper, and roll in the breadcrumbs. ❧ Deep-fry in plenty of very hot oil until golden brown. Drain on paper towels and serve hot.

- 4–6 cardoons
- ½ lemon
- 2½ tablespoons all-purpose/plain flour
- 1 egg, lightly beaten
- salt to taste
- freshly ground black pepper
- 7 tablespoons fine dry breadcrumbs
- extra-virgin olive oil or good quality ordinary olive oil for frying

Suggested wine: a dry rosé
(Etna rosato)

Cardoons (which are closely related to artichokes) have a pleasantly sharp and slightly bitter taste. They are a great favorite in western Sicily where they grow wild. If you can't get cardoons, this recipe will be equally delicious if tender green celery is used in their place. The celery stalks won't need rubbing with lemon and will only require about 10–15 minutes boiling before frying.

Dolci

With its almost inexhaustible variety of desserts, candies, and cakes, Sicily is a paradise for anyone with a sweet tooth. Many of the island's pastrycooks are very skilled, maintaining standards that raise patisserie to an art form, and some of the more traditional recipes, such as Sicilian Cheesecake or Fried Pastries with Ricotta Cheese and Candied Fruit, are fairly challenging. Happily, others, including Zabaglione, Black Rice Pudding, and Lemon Cream, are as simple as they are delicious. This chapter also includes two recipes for crunchy nougat (or toffee brittle), reminding us yet again of Sicily's age-old ties with the Middle East.

Gelu di Muluni

Watermelon Jelly

Sieve or liquidize the watermelon. You should obtain about 4½ cups/1¾ pints/1 liter of sieved watermelon flesh. ❧ Place the prepared watermelon in a large saucepan. Add the sugar, cornstarch, and jasmine water (if using) and heat fairly slowly, stirring well. ❧ When it comes to a boil, reduce the heat and simmer for 4–5 minutes, stirring continuously. ❧ Remove from the heat, add the cinnamon, and leave to cool, but do not chill. Add the candied pumpkin or citron peel and chocolate. ❧ Rinse the inside of a 1 quart/1¾ pint/1 liter capacity mold with cold water and fill with the watermelon mixture. ❧ Chill in the refrigerator for several hours, or until completely set. ❧ Turn out onto a serving dish, decorate with jasmine flowers and serve.

Serves 4
Preparation: 15 minutes
Cooking: 7–8 minutes
Recipe grading: easy

- a 5 lb/2 kg watermelon or piece of freshly cut watermelon, peeled and seeded
- ½ cup/4 oz/125 g sugar
- scant ⅔ cup/2½ oz/75 g cornstarch/cornflour
- 1 tablespoon jasmine flower water (optional)
- dash of ground cinnamon
- 4 tablespoons candied pumpkin, or candied citron peel, diced
- 3 tablespoons chopped or coarsely grated unsweetened chocolate
- fresh jasmine flowers for decoration

Suggested wine: a sweet white
(Moscato di Siracusa)

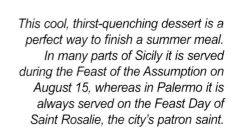

This cool, thirst-quenching dessert is a perfect way to finish a summer meal. In many parts of Sicily it is served during the Feast of the Assumption on August 15, whereas in Palermo it is always served on the Feast Day of Saint Rosalie, the city's patron saint.

Cannoli

Fried Pastries with Ricotta Cheese and Candied Fruit

Preparation: 25 minutes + 1 hour's resting time

Cooking: 30–40 minutes

Recipe grading: complicated

Sift the flour into a bowl and make a well in the center. Drop in the egg yolk and add the sugar, brandy, wine, shortening, and salt. ❧ Mix rapidly, adding more wine if necessary. The dough should be smooth and elastic. ❧ Shape into a ball, wrap in a cloth and set aside for at least 1 hour. ❧ Roll the dough out thinly and cut into 12 squares. ❧ Rub the cannoli tubes with almond oil and wrap the squares diagonally round the tubes, starting with one corner of a square and finishing with the opposite corner. ❧ Lightly beat the egg white and use it to moisten the overlapping surfaces. This will stop them from unwrapping during cooking. ❧ Deep fry, 2–3 at a time, in plenty of very hot shortening or oil, until they are a deep golden brown, with small blisters on the surface. ❧ Lift out with a slotted spoon and drain on paper towels. When cool enough to handle, slide them carefully off the pastry tubes. ❧ Sieve the ricotta into a bowl and beat in the sugar until light and fluffy. ❧ Fold in the chocolate and candied peel. ❧ Fill the cases and dip each end in the nuts. Sift a little confectioners' sugar over them and serve.

- 1½ cups/6 oz/180 g all-purpose/plain flour
- 1 egg, separated
- 2½ tablespoons white granulated or superfine/caster sugar
- 1 tablespoon brandy
- 2½ tablespoons dry white wine or dry Marsala wine
- 2 tablespoons/1 oz/30 g shortening, lard or butter, melted and cooled
- dash of salt
- 3 tablespoons almond oil
- shortening/lard or oil for frying
- 8 oz/250 g fresh ricotta cheese
- 1 cup/4 oz/125 g confectioners'/icing sugar
- ¼ cup/2 oz/60 g very finely diced mixed candied peel (pumpkin, orange, citron)
- 1 square/1 oz/30 g semi-sweet/unsweetened dark chocolate, finely chopped
- 2½ tablespoons peeled and finely chopped pistachio nuts
- confectioners'/icing sugar

Suggested wine: a sweet white (Moscato di Noto)

Always remember to fill the cannoli just before serving or the pastry will become soggy. You will need 12 cannoli metal tubes ¾ in/2 cm in diameter and 6 in/15 cm long. The pastry casings can be made a couple of days in advance and stored in an airtight container.

Serves 4–6
Preparation: 45 minutes
Cooking: 20 minutes
Recipe grading: fairly easy

- butter and potato flour for preparing the molds
- 7 oz/200 g shelled pistachio nuts
- scant 1 cup/7 oz/200 g granulated or superfine/caster sugar
- dash of salt
- 4 eggs, separated
- finely grated zest/rind of 1 medium orange
- ½ cup/2 oz/60 g potato flour

Suggested wine: a sweet white
(Malvasia delle Lipari)

Mazarisi
Pistachio Cakes

Grease and flour the inside of 10–12 little ckae molds (each of about ½ cup/3½ fl oz/100 ml capacity). ∂ To blanch the pistachio nuts, place them in a heatproof bowl and pour boiling water over them. Leave to stand for 1 minute, then drain well. Transfer to a large, clean cloth and rub off their thin, inner skins. ∂ Put the pistachios into a food processor with the sugar and salt, grind them fairly finely, and transfer to a mixing bowl. ∂ Whisk the egg whites until stiff but not dry. ∂ Stir the yolks and orange peel into the pistachio and sugar mixture and mix thoroughly. ∂ Gently fold a little at a time into the whites, alternating with the potato flour sifted directly into the bowl. ∂ Fill each little mold not more than three-quarters full and bake in a preheated oven at 325°F/160°C/gas 3 for 20 minutes. ∂ Turn them out of their molds while still hot and leave to cool completely before serving.

These light, soufflé-type cakes are named after the town of Mazara del Vallo on the west coast of Sicily where they are served on festive occasions. Their outside surface is an ordinary beige color but inside they are the most exquisite delicate green.

Turruni
Nougat

Spread the almonds out in a single layer in a large shallow baking pan and roast in a preheated oven at 400°F/200°C/gas 6 for 5–7 minutes until very pale golden brown. ❧ Set aside to cool. ❧ Oil the baking pan with almond oil ready for later use. ❧ When the almonds have cooled a little, transfer to a chopping board or food processor and chop coarsely (or leave whole, if preferred). ❧ Place the almonds in a large heavy-bottomed saucepan with the sugar and water. Stir over low heat until the sugar melts and caramelizes, turning a light nut brown. ❧ Remove from the heat and, working quickly, stir in the lemon peel and the cinnamon, mixing thoroughly. ❧ Transfer at once to the baking pan and use a spatula dipped in cold water to spread to a thickness of about ½ in/1 cm. ❧ Set aside to cool a little, then cut it into rectangles or squares. ❧ Serve when completely cold. ❧ The nougat will keep well in a dry, airtight container.

Serves 6
Preparation: 10 minutes
Cooking: 10 minutes
Recipe grading: easy

- 3½ cups/1 lb/500 g shelled whole almonds
- generous tablespoon almond oil
- 1¾ cups/14 oz/400 g granulated or superfine/caster sugar
- 3½ tablespoons water
- finely grated zest/rind of ½ lemon
- 1 teaspoon ground cinnamon

Suggested wine: a semi-dry Marsala (Marsala Superiore)

This recipe is much less demanding than the classic version made with honey, which calls for very exact timing. It is no less delicious for being less complicated.

Torrone

A whole book could be dedicated to the delights of Italian *torrone* (a type of nougat). *Torrone* is a candy made from almonds, sugar, and honey (but with many other ingredients too, depending on where it is made), which obviously came from the East, since versions of it can also be found in Greece, Turkey, and many parts of North Africa, and the Middle East. Fresh *torrone* is made each year in the fall as soon as the almonds and other nuts have been harvested. It has become a traditional Christmas treat and Italians place long, gift wrapped bars of it under the tree or serve it with the dried fruit and nuts at the end of the meal during the festive season. The many Sicilian recipes for *torrone* are especially exquisite and elaborate.

Cubbaita, *a soft, chewy* torrone *made with the basic honey, sugar, and almonds, but with the addition of plenty of sesame seeds is perhaps the most typically Sicilian type of* torrone. *The name derives from the Arab word* qubbayta *or* qubbiat, *meaning "with almonds," and betrays the fact that the Arabs introduced* torrone *to the island. Both the sesame seeds and almonds are usually toasted before being mixed into the honey and sugar. Cubbaita is cut into large lozenge shapes or rectangles ³/₄ in/2 cm thick.*

Dried fruit and nuts of all sorts thrive in the mild Sicilian climate. Almonds are the classic ingredient in torrone, *but hazelnuts, pistachio nuts, and peanuts are also used. One type of* torrone, *called* Cicirata, *used to be made in Licata on the southern coast of the island, with roasted fava beans (broad peas) cooked in honey!*

The fragrant Sicilian meadows are ideal for bees and many varieties of honey are produced.

CLASSIC TORRONE

3¹/₂ cups/1 lb/500 g shelled whole almonds

1³/₄ cups/8 oz/250 g shelled whole pistachio nuts

scant 1 cup/10 oz/300 g fairly liquid honey

1¹/₂ cups/10 oz/300 g sugar

scant ¹/₂ cup/3¹/₂ fl oz/100 ml water

3 egg whites

³/₄ cup/3¹/₂ oz/100 g candied orange peel, finely chopped

2 tablespoons grated lemon zest/rind

generous tablespoon of almond oil

Toast the almonds and pistachio nuts in the oven as described on page 101. When light golden brown, remove from the oven and shake vigorously to remove as much of the inner protective skins as possible. ❧ Heat the honey in the top pan of a double boiler. Cook for about 1¹/₂ hours, stirring almost continuously with a wooden spoon until the honey turns a reddy color. At this point, use a teaspoon to scoop out a little of the honey and drop it into cold water; if it hardens quickly and turns almost brittle, it is ready. ❧ While the honey is cooking, melt the sugar and water over a very low heat in another pan. Continue cooking until it gets past the sticky stage. Use a teaspoon to scoop up a little of the mixture and drop it into cold water; if it hardens quickly, becoming almost glass-like, it is ready. ❧ Beat the egg whites until stiff. ❧ While the pan containing the honey is still over the hot water, very carefully fold the egg whites into the honey. Cook for 5 minutes, stirring continuously. The mixture will become bubbly. ❧ Add the sugar and cook for 5 more minutes. When the mixture begins to harden, add the almonds, pistachio nuts, candied orange, and lemon zest and stir until well mixed. ❧ Transfer to a large baking pan, previously oiled with the almond oil. Spread with a spatula and set aside to cool. ❧ When cool, turn out onto a hard surface and cut into rectangles. The *torrone* will keep well if wrapped in parchment paper and stored in an airtight jar.

Cassata
Sicilian Cheese Cake

Serves 6

Preparation: 2 hours + 4–8 hours' chilling

Cooking: 30 minutes

Recipe grading: complicated

- 5 eggs, separated
- $^2/_3$ cup/5 oz/150 g granulated or superfine /caster sugar
- zest/rind of 1 lemon
- generous dash of salt
- 1 cup/4 oz/125 g all-purpose or cake flour/plain or cake flour, sifted
- butter and flour for preparing the pans
- 1 lb/500 g very fresh ricotta cheese
- $1^1/_4$ cups/8 oz/250 g granulated or superfine/caster sugar
- scant $^1/_2$ cup/$3^1/_2$ fl oz/100 ml rum or Maraschino
- generous $^1/_2$ cup/5 oz/150 g diced candied mixed peel
- $3^1/_2$ squares/$3^1/_2$ oz/100 g coarsely grated semi-sweet/unsweetened dark chocolate
- 6 tablespoons sieved apricot jelly or jam
- $1^3/_4$ cups/7 oz/200 g confectioner's/icing sugar, sifted
- 1 egg white
- 2 teaspoons orange flower water
- $1^1/_4$ cups/10 oz/300 g assorted candied fruits

Suggested wine: a dry or semi-dry Marsala (Marsala Superiore)

Beat the egg yolks, sugar, salt, and zest until pale and fluffy. ❧ Whisk the whites until stiff and fold 2–3 heaped tablespoonfuls at a time into the yolks, alternating with the flour. ❧ Transfer the mixture to two greased and floured rectangular bread pans $8^1/_2$ in/22 cm long and bake in a preheated oven at 350°F/180°C/gas 4 for 25–30 minutes. Cool on a rack. ❧ Sieve the ricotta into a bowl, mix in the second measure of sugar and 3 tablespoons of the rum or Maraschino. ❧ Fold in the peel and chocolate. ❧ Line an 8–9 in/20–22 cm diameter round dish with greaseproof or nonstick baking paper and spread all over with a thin layer of jam. ❧ Slice the sponge thinly and drizzle with the remaining rum mixed with 1 tablespoon water. ❧ Line the base and sides of the dish with most of the sponge pieces and fill with the ricotta, smoothing the top. ❧ Cover with the last pieces of sponge, fitting them together closely but not overlapping. ❧ Chill in the refrigerator for 2–6 hours. ❧ Carefully turn the cassata out onto a serving plate and peel off the lining paper. ❧ Heat the remaining jam a little and spread over the surface. ❧ Set aside to cool. ❧ Mix the confectioners' sugar with the egg white and the orange flower water and spread smoothly over the cassata. ❧ Decorate with the candied fruits and chill in the refrigerator for at least 2 hours before serving. ❧ For a traditional green frosting (icing), add a few drops of green food coloring to the egg white and confectioner's sugar so that it turns a pale, pistachio green. ❧ For an extra rich cassata, cover the sides of the cake with royal almond paste colored pistachio green.

Pignulata

Snow on the Mountain Dessert

Separate two of the eggs, place the whites in a large bowl, and set aside for the frosting. ❧ Sift the flour into a large mixing bowl. ❧ Make a well in the center, break in the remaining egg, and add the yolks, all but 1 tablespoon of the butter, the salt, and brandy. ❧ Gradually work these ingredients into the flour, first with a fork, then by hand until the dough is smooth and elastic. ❧ Divide the dough into 4 or 5 portions and roll each into a long cylinder about as thick as a finger. Cut into slices ½ in/1 cm thick. ❧ Grease a baking sheet with the remaining butter and bake the pieces of dough in a preheated oven at 350°F/180°C/gas 4 for 15 minutes, or until they are pale golden brown. ❧ Remove from the oven and set aside to cool. ❧ To make the frosting, add the sifted confectioners' sugar and lemon juice to the egg whites and mix until smooth. ❧ Set aside 7 tablespoons of this frosting in a small bowl. ❧ Working fast (so that the frosting doesn't have time to set), add the baked dough pieces to the icing left in the large bowl and stir gently to coat all over. ❧ Divide the mixture into 4–6 portions and heap it up on confectioners' or ice cream wafers, cut into squares or disks. ❧ Spoon some of the extra frosting over each one. ❧ Set aside for several hours before serving.

Serves 4–6
Preparation: 20 minutes + several hours' standing
Cooking: 15 minutes
Recipe grading: fairly easy

- 3 eggs
- 2 cups/8 oz/250 g all-purpose/plain flour
- ½ cup/4 oz/125 g butter, softened and cut into small pieces
- generous dash of salt
- 3 tablespoons brandy
- 3½ cups/14 oz/400 g confectioners'/icing sugar
- 4 teaspoons lemon juice

Suggested wine: a sweet white (Moscato di Noto)

The Italian name for this dessert comes from the word pigna, *meaning "pine cone", which is what each finished dessert should look like. There are many versions: this one comes from Messina and is probably the most well known outside Italy.*

Zabaione
Zabaglione

Serves 4
Preparation: 5 minutes
Cooking: 10 minutes
Recipe grading: easy

- 4 egg yolks
- ½ cup/2 oz/60 g granulated/caster sugar
- scant ½ cup/3½ fl oz/100 ml dry Marsala

Combine the egg yolks and sugar in the top pan of a double boiler (not on the heat yet) and whisk until they are pale yellow and creamy. ❧ Add the Marsala gradually, beating continuously, then place the pan in the bottom pan of the double boiler over warm water and cook, beating continuously with the whisk, until the mixture thickens. ❧ Keep the heat extremely low so that the zabaglione does not boil or it will curdle. ❧ Serve warm or cold. If serving cold, cover with plastic wrap (clingfilm) so that it is touching the surface to prevent a skin from forming as the mixture cools.

Zabaglione is now popular all over Italy, although the fact that its distinguishing ingredient is Marsala would seem to point to Sicilian origins. Serve in glass cups by itself, or spoon it over bowls of fresh, diced raw fruit or pieces of chopped plain sponge cake.

Granita di Caffè
Coffee Ice with Whipped Cream

Dissolve the sugar in the hot, freshly made coffee, then stir in the water. ✍ Transfer the mixture to a large ice tray or bowl and place in the freezer for 3–4 hours. Stir the mixture about once every 20 minutes so that it doesn't become solid but freezes as crystals of ice. ✍ Remove from the freezer about 30 minutes before serving and spoon into individual serving bowls. ✍ Whip the cream with the confectioners' sugar until stiff and spoon in equal portions over the coffee ice.

Serves 6

Preparation: 10 minutes + 3–4 hours' freezing

Cooking: 10 minutes

Recipe grading: easy

- ¾ cup/6 oz/180 g granulated /caster sugar
- scant ½ cup/3½ fl oz/100 ml strong black coffee (preferably espresso)
- 2 cups/16 fl oz/500 ml water
- 1 cup/8 fl oz/250 ml heavy/double cream
- 2 tablespoons confectioners'/icing sugar

Granita makes a refreshing dessert, especially at the end of a large meal on a hot summer's night. In Sicily, however, it was traditionally served together with a light brioche at breakfast.

Biancomangiare

Lemon Cream

Serves 4–6

Preparation: 15 minutes + 2 hours' chilling

Cooking: 10 minutes

Recipe grading: easy

- ½ cup/4 oz/125 g superfine or granulated/caster sugar
- 1 cup/4 oz/125 g all-purpose/plain flour
- grated zest/rind of 2 lemons
- 4¼ cups/1¾ pints/1 liter whole/full cream milk

Combine the sugar, flour, and zest of 1 lemon in a heavy-bottomed pan. Gradually stir in the milk, making sure that no lumps form. ✄ Place the pan over a medium-low heat and, stirring continuously, bring to a boil. ✄ Boil for 1 minute, then remove from the heat. ✄ Pour into a mold and leave to cool. When cool place in the refrigerator for at least 2 hours. ✄ Serve cold sprinkled with the remaining grated lemon zest.

This recipe can be varied to make other delicious creams: replace the lemon zest with 2 tablespoons of unsweetened cocoa powder for Chocolate Cream, or with an egg yolk and a few drops of vanilla extract (essence) for Vanilla Cream.

Vucciddatu

Candied Fruit Ring

Mix the flour, butter, sugar, 1 egg, salt, and about half the Marsala together in a bowl to obtain a firm, smooth dough. ❧ Wrap in a clean dish cloth and set aside to rest for about 2 hours. ❧ Chop the almonds, figs, chocolate, pistachio nuts, and walnuts together and place in a heavy-bottomed pan with the cinnamon, lemon zest, and the remaining Marsala. ❧ Cook over low heat for about 10 minutes, stirring frequently. Set aside to cool. ❧ Roll out the dough in a rectangular shape until it is about ½ in/1 cm thick. ❧ Spread the cooled fruit mixture over the dough and roll up. Join the ends of the roll to form a ring and seal so that no filling comes out during cooking. ❧ Carefully transfer the ring to a buttered or oiled baking sheet and bake in a preheated oven at 400°F/200°C/gas 6 for about 25 minutes. ❧ Beat the egg yolk with a whisk. ❧ Remove the ring from the oven and brush with the egg yolk. Return to the oven and cook for 5 minutes. ❧ Turn off the oven and leave the ring in the oven until cool. ❧ Serve at room temperature.

Serves 6

Preparation: 30 minutes + 2 hours' resting

Cooking: 45 minutes

Recipe grading: fairly easy

- 3½ cups/12 oz/350 g flour
- ⅔ cup/5 oz/150 g butter, softened
- ⅓ cup/3½ oz/100 g sugar
- 1 egg + 1 yolk
- dash of salt
- scant ½ cup/3½ fl oz/100 ml dry Marsala
- ⅔ cup/3½ oz/100 g almonds, toasted
- 1½ cups/8 oz/250 g dried figs
- 3½ squares/3½ oz/100 g semi-sweet/unsweetened dark chocolate
- ⅓ cup/2 oz/60 g pistachio nuts
- ⅓ cup/2 oz/60 g shelled walnuts
- dash of ground cinnamon
- grated zest/rind of 1 lemon

Suggested wine: a dry or semi-dry Marsala (Marsala Superiore)

This nourishing ring makes an excellent snack or a hearty dessert during the cold winter months. Feel free to vary the types and mixtures of fruit and spices, or replace the chocolate with the same quantity of honey.

Riso Nero
Black Rice Pudding

Serves 6
Preparation: 5 minutes
Cooking: 25 minutes
Recipe grading: easy

Heat the milk and sugar in a heavy-bottomed pan over medium-low heat. ❧ When the milk is boiling, add the rice and cook for about 20 minutes, or until the rice is well-cooked and the milk has all been absorbed. Depending on the quality of the rice, you may need to add a little more milk during cooking or strain a little milk off the mixture when the rice is cooked. ❧ Add three-quarters of the chocolate and the cinnamon and stir until well mixed. ❧ Remove from heat and pour into a deep serving bowl. Sprinkle with the remaining chocolate and serve while still warm.

- 4½ cups/1¾ pints/1 liter whole/full cream milk
- ⅓ cup/3½ oz/100 g sugar
- 2¼ cups/1 lb/500 g rice (preferably Italian Arborio rice)
- 7 squares/7 oz/200 g semi-sweet/unsweetened dark chocolate, grated
- dash of ground cinnamon

This wonderful dessert is definitely winter fare.
It is particularly good served with whipped cream.

Index

Acknowledgments

The Publishers would like to thank Mastrociliegia, Fiesole (Florence) who kindly lent props for photography.

All photos by MARCO LANZA except:

GIULIANO CAPPELLI, FLORENCE: COVER (LANDSCAPE), BACK COVER (B), 3, 7, 11B, 12T, 13T, 20B; FARABOLAFOTO, MILAN: 1, 2, 6, 8 (M. DI STEFANO), 12B (F. PESCI), 13B (M. DI STEFANO), 21TL, 21B, 34B, 35T, 35B, 38 (M. LANFRANCHI), 40T, 40BL, 40BR, 41T, 41B, 53T, 53B, 70T, 71B, 94T, 106B, 107T; MELO MINNELLA, PALERMO: BACK COVER (T), 9, 11T, 21R, 52, 70B, 71T, 83T, 100, 106T; ADRIANO NARDI, FLORENCE: BACK COVER (CR), 58, 82T, 82B; ARCHIVIO SCALA: 5